MEDIATION IN A TIME OF CRISIS

MEDIATION IN A TIME OF CRISIS

PANDEMIC, PREJUDICE, POLICE, AND POLITICAL POLARIZATION

KENNETH CLOKE

BOOKS BY KENNETH CLOKE

Mediation: Revenge and the Magic of Forgiveness, Center for Dispute Resolution, Santa Monica, California, 1996

Mediating Dangerously: The Frontiers of Conflict Resolution, Jossey Bass/Wiley Publishers Inc., 2001

The Crossroads of Conflict: A Journey into the Heart of Dispute Resolution, Janis Publishers Inc., 2006

Conflict Revolution: Mediating Evil, War, Injustice and Terrorism, Janis Publishers Inc., 2008

The Dance of Opposites: Explorations in Mediation, Dialogue and Conflict Resolution Systems Design, GoodMedia Press, 2014

Conflict Revolution: Designing Preventative Systems for Chronic Social, Economic and Political Conflicts, (Second Edition) GoodMedia Press, 2015

Politics, Dialogue and the Evolution of Democracy: How to Discuss Race, Abortion, Immigration Gun Control, Climate Change, Same Sex Marriage and Other Hot Topics, GoodMedia Press, 2018

Words of Wisdom: Profound, Poignant and Provocative Quotes for Your Insight and Inspiration, GoodMedia Press, 2018

Ordinary Ecstasy: A Meditation Home Companion, Center for Dispute Resolution, 2018

The Crossroads of Conflict: A Journey into the Heart of Dispute Resolution, (Second Edition) GoodMedia Press, 2019

BOOKS BY KENNETH CLOKE AND JOAN GOLDSMITH

Thank God It's Monday: 14 Values We Need to Humanize the Way We Work, Irwin/McGraw Hill, 1997

Resolving Conflicts at Work: A Complete Guide for Everyone on the Job, Jossey Bass/Wiley Publishers Inc., 2000

Resolving Personal and Organizational Conflicts: Stories of Transformation and Forgiveness, Jossey Bass/Wiley Publishers Inc., 2000

The End of Management and the Rise of Organizational Democracy, Jossey Bass/Wiley Publishers Inc., 2002

The Art of Waking People Up: Cultivating Awareness and Authenticity at Work, Jossey Bass/Wiley Publishers Inc., 2003

Resolving Conflicts at Work: Eight Strategies for Everyone on the Job (Second Edition) Jossey Bass/Wiley Publishers Inc., 2005

Resolving Conflicts at Work: Ten Strategies for Everyone on the Job (Third Edition) Jossey Bass/Wiley Publishers Inc., 2011

Resolving Organizational Conflicts: A Course on Mediation and Systems Design, GoodMedia Press, 2021

Re-Designing the Way We Work: A Guide to Living with Pandemic, Climate Change, and Political Conflict, to be published, 2022

CONTENTS

GoodMedia Press
An imprint of GoodMedia Communications, LLC
25 Highland Park Village, 100-810
Dallas, Texas 75205
www.goodmediapress.com

Book cover and book layout design by GoodMedia Press.
The text in this book is set in Crimson Text.

Manufactured in USA

Publisher's Cataloging-in-Publication data

Names: Cloke, Kenneth, 1941-, author.
Title: Mediation in a time of crisis : pandemic , prejudice , police , and political polarization / Kenneth Cloke.
Description: Includes index. I Dallas, TX: GoodMedia Press, 2021.
Identifiers: LCCN: 2021950235 I ISBN: 979-8-9852429-0-4 (print) I 979-8-9852429-2-8 (ebook)
Subjects: LCSH Conflict management. I Mediation. I Dispute resolution (Law)--United States. I Negotiation--United States. I COVID-19 (Disease)--United States--21st century. I I United States--Race relations--21st century. I Police-community relations--United States--21st century. I United States--Social conditions--21st century. I Political culture--United States. I United States--Politics and government--21st century--Moral and ethical aspects. I United States--Politics and government--2017- I BISAC LAW / Alternative Dispute Resolution I LAW / Arbitration, Negotiation, Mediation I POLITICAL SCIENCE / Civil Rights I POLITICAL SCIENCE / Political Ideologies I POLITICAL SCIENCE / Religion, Politics & State I SOCIAL SCIENCE / Discrimination I SOCIAL SCIENCE / Violence in Society
Classification: LCC KF9084 .C56 2021 I DDC 347.73/9--dc23

How do we hold people accountable for wrongdoing and yet at the same time remain in touch with their humanity enough to believe in their capacity to be transformed.

— BELL HOOKS

The sea rises, the light fails, lovers cling to each other, and children cling to us. The moment we cease to hold each other, the moment we break faith with one another, the sea engulfs us and the light goes out.

— JAMES BALDWIN

The trouble is, you think you have time.

— JACK KORNFIELD

—

INTRODUCTION

CONFLICTS, CRISES, AND POLITICAL EVOLUTION

The political class ... is strategically incapable of addressing even short-term crises, let alone a vast existential predicament.... Those who govern the nation and shape public discourse cannot be trusted with the preservation of life on Earth. There is no benign authority preserving us from harm. No one is coming to save us. None of us can justifiably avoid the call to come together to save ourselves.

— GEORGE MONBIOT

The whole of public policy is an attempt to reconstitute a culture, a social system, an economic order, that have in fact reached their end, reached their limits of viability. And then I sit here and look at this double inevitability; that this imperial, exporting, divided order is ending, and that all its residual forces, all its political formations, will fight to the end to reconstruct it, to re-establish it, moving deeper all the time through crisis after crisis in an impossible attempt to regain a familiar world. So then a double inevitability: that they will fail, and that they will try nothing else.

— RAYMOND WILLIAMS

Adventure is a crisis that one accepts, crisis is an adventure that one refuses. And it is possible at every moment in our life, to decide whether the rupture that comes upon us is here to destroy us or to make us evolve, to force us to find in ourselves resources that we didn't know could exist.

— BERTRAND PICCARD

We have entered an era of escalating conflicts and crises, in which our survival as a civilization and as a species, increasingly depend — not on military prowess, economic might, or political dominance — but on our ability to listen empathetically, communicate non-violently, solve problems jointly, negotiate collaboratively, decide consensually, act collectively, and resolve conflicts meditatively.

They therefore depend also on our capacity to appreciate diversity and dissent, engage in dialogue with those who think differently, and build trust between former foes; on our ability to bridge and dismantle the social, economic, political, cultural, and environmental barriers we have erected over centuries to dominate and prevail over others.

Chief among these barriers is the *form* of our politics, our governments and nation states, which have historically served and defended unequal social, economic, and political systems that are grounded in domination, privilege, and prejudice; that rank social improvement, public health, environmental sustainability, human life, and even *survival* as less important than private wealth, profitability, destructive growth, and competitive advantage.

As a result, we are facing intensifying conflicts and crises around the world that pit popular demand for solutions to a growing number of escalating problems against the wealthy elites, corporate giants, bureaucracies, and political institutions that created, exacerbated, ignored, tolerated, covered up, and profited from them, in part by paying political leaders to deny and discount them.

What is worse, the nation state *itself*, perhaps the most powerful problem solving mechanism ever created, has become an obstacle, partly because the problems and crises we increasingly confront exceed its bounds, and are now global in scope. Sovereignty and nationalism more and more stand in the way of transnational communication, cooperation, and consensus. As a result, local politicians find it nearly impossible to address the general, global, species-interests of all — *except* selfishly, competitively, adversarially, and in ways that defeat or diminish global cooperation.

At the same time, global cooperation by means of the nation state is *essential* in attempting to solve these problems. Without some form of international problem solving that is vastly stronger than individual states or the presently constituted United Nations is able to muster; and without widespread adoption of a broad range of transnational collaborative, consensus-building, and conflict resolution methodologies, global problems will increasingly go unsolved, conflicts will fester, divisions will deepen, and these will likely, at some point, connect, creating larger, *general*, universal, fundamental crises that may threaten our survival.

Breakdown Precedes Breakthrough

There are, I believe, two varieties of general, universal, or fundamental crises: one is terminal, leading to ever-deeper dysfunctions, and ending simply in extinction. The other leads to evolution, transformation, and the emergence of higher, *emergent* forms of order. The second can be seen in nature in phase transitions, as when water turns into ice, or fissionable material produces a chain reaction, or a magnetic material is heated and loses its magnetism, or cellular automata generate complex, unforeseen patterns.

As these phase transitions begin, the material or substance enters a state of "criticality," in which beginning and end states coexist, new systems self-organize in isolated pockets or random interstices, and complexity increases exponentially, giving rise both to chaos, and to newly emergent, higher order phenomena. Then, fractal self-similarity or scale invariance, higher degrees of freedom or dimensionality, and power laws begin to emerge at the critical points *between* phases, resolving the crisis locally, and easing the transition of the whole material into a new state.

The nature of this new, higher state of organization is initially tiny, disconnected, and unremarkable, but as it begins to expand, it creates islands of stability and order while the older, lower order state slips deeper into chaos and disorder. Chaos is then *exported* through complex, self-organizing systems and dissipative structures, as described chemist and Nobel laureate Ilya Prigogine in *Order Out of Chaos*.

In a similar way, in human conflicts, the emergence of order out of chaos is often eased or facilitated by mediation, which plays the role of catalyst in the transformation of lower order attitudes, skills, communications, processes, relationships, systems, structures, cultures, etc., into higher order ones that are capable of learning from conflicts and crises how to transform the information they contain into the self-organization of social cooperation, collaborative problem solving, and evolution to higher order conflicts and crises.

Rainer Maria Rilke wrote, "The future enters into us, in order to transform itself in us, long before it happens." Similarly, we are able to find, in times of crisis and intractable conflict, the very higher order skills that are needed in order to overcome them. These skills steadily grow inside, between, and around us as our conflicts deepen and crises become chaotic.

What are these higher order skills? They include, at their core, the ability to listen and empathize with those who are different; to work together to solve common problems; to engage in dialogue over disagreements; to build consensus; to negotiate collaboratively; to mediate conflicts, and to seek restorative justice in unifying and empowering solutions.

In these ways, it becomes possible to face the conflicts and crises created by the global pandemic, prejudice, policing, polarization, along with insurrection, climate change, environmental devastation, and similar problems together, minimize their destructive effects, evolve to higher forms of social, economic, and political relationship, and hopefully, at some point, stop slaughtering, hating, and dominating one another.

About this Book

Starting in 2019 and continuing into 2020 and 21, a rapid convergence of issues, events, conflicts, and crises began, pointing toward dramatically different futures. From the primaries and Presidential elections to the insurrection on January 6; from the deaths and devastation caused by the pandemic to impassioned resistance to masks and vaccines; from the murders of George Floyd and Brionna Taylor to the rise of white supremacy and Black Lives Matter; from sexual harassment and #metoo to Jeffrey Epstein, Harvey Weinstein, and Andrew Cuomo; from unprecedented fires, floods, and heat waves to business-as-usual and climate change denial; from war and civilian casualties in Afghanistan, Somalia, Yemen, Israel and the Palestinian Territories to continued hostilities with Russia, China, Iran, and others, we have faced unprecedented conflicts and crises that require unprecedented solutions.

In response to these seemingly intractable conflicts and crises, I wrote the chapters in this book, more or less in chronological order, in an effort to explore how mediation techniques, conflict resolution insights, and collaborative methodologies might be adapted, scaled-up, and set to work. The chapters that follow are therefore both a chronicle of unfolding events, which I have left exactly as I described them at the time, without editing or hindsight; and a set of practical proposals on how to apply these ideas and principles.

Some of the ideas and proposals that follow were first discussed and developed in earlier books I have written, especially in *The Dance of Opposites: Explorations in Mediation, Dialogue, and Systems Design* (2014); *Conflict Revolution: Designing Preventative Systems for Chronic Social, Economic and Political Conflicts*, (2015); and *Politics, Dialogue and the Evolution of Democracy: How to Discuss Race, Abortion, Immigration Gun Control, Climate Change, Same Sex Marriage and Other Hot Topics*, (2018).

Many of the chapters that follow are brief, practical, and directed at specific conflicts, while others are longer, more abstract, and attempts to gain clarity regarding complex, multifaceted ideas and principles. Some were circulated on Mediate.com, or appeared in other books, which are cited. All are attempts to shift the way we think and act in times of conflict and crisis, and to encourage the adaptation and application of conflict resolution skills and techniques to the social, economic, political, and environmental disputes and crises that impact us.

We can no longer afford to waste time, energy, lives, money, and precious resources on needlessly fighting with each other, especially when a few simple, inexpensive, easily implemented conflict resolution processes will allow us to be far more successful and far less cruel to one another. The stakes are high and getting higher, and mediation has proven successful in countless conflicts over similar issues in all cultures and communities. The old ways are failing and new ones are needed. Our conflicts and crises are not over, and will not wait. Whatever each of us can offer, even if wrong, will help us discover better ways of living together and solving common problems.

Kenneth Cloke

Santa Monica, California

WHAT WE CAN LEARN FROM THE PANDEMIC

Suddenly, in a moment, everything has shifted. Unimaginable outcomes are now revealed as mere habits, assumptions, patterns of thought, feeling, and behavior —driven by an unquestioning desire for comfort and security, and a fear of what we do not know. These then limit, channel, and recycle our perceptions, leading us to see as solid what is actually liquid or gaseous.

What matters now, after health and survival, are vision and values, and a willingness to think deeply and creatively about what we have witnessed and experienced – not simply the suffering and loss of life, but also the singing, dancing and celebration of life, the courage and deep desire for connection, the importance of love and collaboration that are taking place everywhere, every day, in the midst of all this loss.

On the one hand, we are deeply divided from one another by this virus – nationally, racially, culturally, religiously, politically —even individually, through fear and social distancing. On the other hand, we are united by it, as all humanity now faces the same problem, and must learn and practice higher order collaboration and conflict resolution skills in order to survive it.

The logic of division is fear and hatred of others, of narrow nationalism and egotism that regard other people as threats to our survival. The logic of unity is love and caring for one another, of globalism and altruism that experience others as essential to our own survival – not just physically, but mentally, emotionally, and spiritually; socially, economically, and politically. These different responses lead to fundamentally different outcomes.

Just imagine what would happen if all the doctors and nurses, farmers and grocery workers, scientists and firemen, decided to stop working and just look out for themselves – and the result is the same, on a smaller scale, for each of us.

Fortunately, most of us are not required to interact personally at close range with those who may be infected with the virus, so our courage and dedication need to take a different form. We can, for example, resist xenophobic efforts to label this the "Chinese virus;" offer our services as mediators, facilitators, and conflict coaches to first responders; agree to work on-line at no or reduced fee with couples, families and organizations in nations and communities that have been locked down; and continue to keep alive the idea that social distancing does not have to mean social isolation, and can be counter-balanced by song and story, and everyday celebrations of empathy and heroism.

We can even *thank* the virus, for reminding us of what is precious; for forcing us to realize that without the courage of health care workers and grocery clerks we would not survive; for asking us to have the courage not to abandon each other, not to put joy and happiness on life support, and not to lose sight of the higher order visions and values we are now being asked to live by.

These are the visions and values of species solidarity, of global cooperation and coordination, of sharing and supporting one another, of valuing our differences and abandoning no one. They are the visions and values of dialogue and collaboration, mediation and negotiation, forgiveness and restorative justice, empathy and mindfulness, love and kindness.

So let us honor the dead and dying, the heroes in hospital gowns and grocery aprons – and let us commit that their sacrifices shall not have been in vain, but dedicate ourselves to turning these otherwise marginalized and sidelined insights in the direction of *global* problem solving. In the end, it doesn't matter whose end of the boat is sinking — with pandemics, as with global warming and environmental degradation, we sink or swim together.

2

SOME LESSONS FROM THE PANDEMIC

If we want things to stay as they are, things will have to change.

— GIUSEPPE TOMASI DI LAMPEDUSA

Every day silence harvests its victims. Silence is a mortal illness.

— NATALIA GINZBURG

Everything has changed, except the way we think.

— ALBERT EINSTEIN (ON HEARING OF THE BOMBING
OF HIROSHIMA)

There are many ways of understanding or defining conflict, each leading to a different set of techniques and approaches, and among them are these, reinforced by our experience of the pandemic:

- Conflict is the lack of appreciation of the imminence of death or sudden catastrophe.

- Conflict is the sound made by the cracks in a system.
- Conflict is a need to evolve, together with a refusal to change.

We have learned from the pandemic that we are all facing death, and are therefore one, connected by crisis and undivided by conflict. And we have also learned that we are facing it differently, and are therefore many, separated by race, gender, nationality, age, religion, wealth, occupation, social class, political beliefs, emotional vulnerability, and physical well being, and divided by conflict.

What we have not learned sufficiently or everywhere is how to turn our differences into deeper and more powerful expressions of empathy and compassion; how to strengthen I/Thou communications and relationships with our opponents; how to use the pandemic to repair the cracks in our systems; and how to evolve to higher *orders* of conflict that reveal and require higher orders of resolution.

We have learned that we can withdraw from the world and still be in it. We have learned to be socially and emotionally connected while physically distant. We have learned the importance of science, and the equal importance of art, music, and dance. We have learned that we can be courageous, even when we are frightened. We have learned the meaning of touch, contact, intimacy, and connection; of having time to reflect, exercise and meditate; of the centrality of celebration and loss. We have learned the depth, extent and intricacy of our interdependency. We have learned the value of slowness, and that when we stop even for a moment, our skies clear of pollution, global warming slows its pace, whales and dolphins return to our shores, and we are able to take pleasure in the beauty of nature and each other.

We have learned that global problems cannot be solved using national or local methods; that death and loss touch all of us; that political conflicts can be deadly; and that it doesn't matter whose end of the boat is sinking. We have learned that it is easier to face death together, even if each of us dies alone, and that looking out for ourselves requires us to look out for each other.

What we have not yet learned is how to hold on to these lessons and not return to an addictive cycle that leads only to future crises and conflicts. We have not learned how to love one another enduringly, or that in all the conflicts we experience between "Us" and "Them," there simply *is* no them, there is only us. We have not, in short, learned the most fundamental lesson in all of conflict resolution: that *every one* of our conflicts contains opportunities for learning, discovery of self and other, and evolution to higher, better, and more satisfying relationships. And that the pandemic is pointing our attention precisely toward those outcomes.

Doing so will require us to bring conflict resolution *directly* into the political arena. It will require us to strengthen global collaboration through dialogue, negotiation and mediation; to invent interest-based forms of political discourse, economic activity, and social problem solving; and to find new ways of assuaging the pathological belief in medical conspiracy, suicidal resistance to common sense health measures, hostility to science and art, and fear and rage toward migrants and minorities that are also infecting us.

None of this will be easy or quick. But, as mediators, we have been silent, confused, reactive, and avoidant in applying our skills and knowledge of conflict resolution to the chronic social, economic and political conflicts that are impacting our response to Covid-19, and to other, equally pressing issues, for far too long, and are paying the price.

So let us honor the dead and dying, the heroes in hospital gowns and grocery aprons, the friends and families who have suffered – and let us commit that their sacrifices shall not have been in vain, by dedicating ourselves, our energies and intentions, our knowledge and skills, to keeping these lessons alive until we have transformed them into renewed hope for a better world, and return — not to our old, conflicted lives, but newer, more collaborative ones, enriched by learning – and not just back, but better.

VISITATION DURING THE
PANDEMIC – WHAT IS CHANGING

I wrote this case study to describe not only how the pandemic impacted the people with whom I was mediating, but how it also changed the way I mediated. The brief summary that follows was published in Michael Lang and Peter Nicholson's book, Living Together, Separating, Divorcing: Surviving During a Pandemic.

I recently received an email from the teenage daughter of a couple whose divorce I mediated several years ago:

Hi Ken! It's Sarah. I hope you are well in this crazy time. I've been thinking about my parent's divorce a lot. As I've mentioned before, I want to live with my mom but the court decided my sister and I would live with both parents. I love my dad but I want some stability. I don't want to move from house to house, especially now with the virus. I want to have one bed at my mom's house. Like you suggested, I wrote a letter addressed to my father. I haven't given it to him because I'm scared. I don't want my sister to feel that I've betrayed her, I don't want my father to bring our family back to court, and I don't want everything to work out just to find out that

having me full time is too hard on my mom. Besides these concerns, I
think I am ready and I want your input. Thank you, Sarah

I have now become Sarah's conflict coach, helping her write to her
father and communicate with her sister and mother without
triggering conflicts.

Many have requested mediation because their kids now have to be
home-schooled and only one parent can monitor their studies during
the week; or one is a doctor on the front lines of the pandemic who
could infect the children; or one wants to leave a pandemic hotspot
and take the kids to live with her elderly parents in a safer rural area;
or an ex-wife has decided to live in quarantine with her new
boyfriend and his kids, and the ex-husband is both jealous and
frightened, and written threatening emails to the new boyfriend.

In each of these cases, I am taking on new roles that supplement and
often overshadow the ones I play in mediation – not only "conflict
coach," but "hostage negotiator," "family shuttle diplomat," "multi-
party consensus builder," "home-schooling educational consultant,"
"pandemic quarantine advisor," and "family dialogue facilitator."

All of this is emotionally intense, with life and death consequences.
And none of it is face-to-face. Zoom is a lifesaver, but it is distant,
untouching, and less immediate and heartfelt than being in the same
room. So many challenges, so much at stake, so little time.

THE MEDIATOR AS LEADER AND THE LEADER AS MEDIATOR:

BUILDING DEMOCRATIC, UBIQUITOUS, COLLABORATIVE LEADERSHIP SKILLS

This chapter was written with Joan Goldsmith. It was subsequently edited and combined with ideas from other mediators, and included in Michael Leathes collection: 17 Keys to Unlock Mediation's Golden Age.

Democracy, as a collaborative form of self-government, uniquely invites *everyone* to participate in leadership, and "followership" as well. Because democracies thrive on diversity, they require leaders who can bring diverse ideas, talents, perspectives, cultures, values, and constituencies together to form an integrated, dynamic, collaborative whole. Democracies need leaders who stand *with*, not over, above, or against those who *choose* whether to follow.

For this reason, democracies — whether in couples, families, teams, groups, neighborhoods, organizations or governments — require leaders who can listen, empower others, generate trust, build relationships, negotiate collaboratively, and resolve conflicts— *ubiquitous* leaders who can follow and build consensus. Democratic leaders are therefore mediators, and mediators are democratic leaders.

Unlike hierarchical, bureaucratic and autocratic forms of leadership, democratic leadership is exercised not only at the top, but at the bottom and throughout. Like mediation, it seeks to balance power and challenges the very *existence* of top and bottom. In democracies, as in mediation, everyone needs to become a responsible, collaborative leader, a team member who helps run the show.

Democratic leaders embody a commitment to values, ethics, and integrity. They inspire collaboration, stimulate synergistic connections, support honest interactions, build trusting relationships, and encourage self-management, diversity, and integration across boundaries. Democratic leaders connect people through problem solving, dialogue, and collaboration so they can intelligently seek solutions. They synthesize diverse approaches, theories, orientations, and discoveries; spark innovation, and create synergies that strengthen consensus and inspire collaboration.

Leadership is a skill. It is not inborn, dependent on money, power, or titles. It is something everyone does at multiple points throughout their lives, whether they consider themselves leaders or not. We all have led someone somewhere sometime, and can do it again — consciously, collaboratively, and effectively. Here is how.

Some skills, behaviors, and traits can be directed or mandated by others, such as attendance ("Be here at 8:00 A.M."), sequential actions ("Do this first and that second"), politeness ("Don't yell"), and repetitive movements ("Tighten this nut").

But there are others that cannot be mandated, lie entirely beyond autocracy's reach, and must instead be led, facilitated, encouraged, supported, mediated, mentored, or coached. See the examples on the following page:

Trust	Consensus
Love	Understanding
Caring	Craftsmanship
Dedication	Wisdom
Creativity	Values
Self-management	Passion
Curiosity	Perseverance
Honesty	Forgiveness
Insight	Initiative
Courage	Unity
Synergy	Flow
Empathy	Trustworthiness
Integrity	Collaboration
Compassion	Follow-through

These are the most important elements in every relationship. Yet hierarchy, bureaucracy and autocracy — whether in families, organizations or governments — interfere with all of them. This does not mean creativity and trust cannot be enhanced, but they cannot be commanded, controlled, ordered, predicted, mandated, regulated, administered, or required, because they depend on spontaneous, voluntary, unregulated, collaborative, *democratic* activity, on choice, and on play.

All democratic relationships require a combination of diversity, consensus, dialogue, teamwork, and mediation to encourage participation in problem solving and decision-making — including picking leaders, not alone but with often a need for courageous, unpopular leadership, which is not always ubiquitous, mediative, or democratic.

We distinguish three styles of leadership: *autocratic*, hierarchical, controlling leaders who take responsibility and make decisions for others; *anarchic*, bureaucratic, detached leaders who administer but abdicate responsibility and let others take the blame; and *democratic*, ubiquitous, collaborative, mediative leaders who inspire, encourage, empower, facilitate, critique, and support.

Democratic leadership is diverse not only in race, gender, age, culture, and sexual orientation, but in experiences, perceptions, thinking preferences, problem solving abilities, communication styles, emotional makeups, and personalities. The primary competencies of leadership, identified by Warren Bennis and Joan Goldsmith in *Learning to Lead*, (#6 was added by us) are:

1. *Mastering The Context:* Understanding the big picture, considering political, economic, social issues, along with science and art; and taking time to learn.
2. *Knowing Ourselves:* Being aware of neurophysiological patterns and our own issues that are triggered by people in conflict; understanding our limits and skills.
3. *Creating Visions and Communicating Meaningfully:* Focusing on the future, having an inspiring vision and being able to communicate it so others can align and collaboratively implement it.
4. *Empowering Others through Empathy, Integrity and Constancy:* Building trust through empathy, empowerment, unconditional integrity, and congruence in beliefs and actions.
5. *Realizing Intentions through Action:* Turning visions into practical solutions, commitment, and strategy; realizing intentions through action.
6. *Preventing and Resolving Conflicts through Collaboration:* Preventing and resolving conflicts through systems design, consensus, collaboration, and shared values.

The skills of democratic mediator-leaders, we believe, coalesce into five different configurations:

1. *Linking Integrity with Behavior: Skills in Leading by Values:* Leading by values means empowering others, encouraging self-management, and helping people define and express

themselves in diverse ways. It means building trust, communicating honestly and empathetically, and inspiring personal commitment. It means being true to one's self.

2. *Linking Change with Ideas: Skills in Revolutionary Thinking:* Revolutionary thinking begins with utopian vision, and seeks to translate it into reality. It means being open to ideas that fundamentally critique existing paradigms and seeking to transform them. It therefore originates in conflicts, anomalies, mistakes, disharmonies, and problems, and the sounds made by the cracks in a system.

3. *Linking Feelings with Balance: Skills in Emotional Intelligence:* Democratic, collaborative, mediative leadership requires emotional intelligence because everyone is emotional, and all relationships need to be designed with human beings in mind.

4. *Linking People with Each Other: Skills in Relationship Building:* Relationship skills are needed to balance unity and diversity, deepen trust and mutual support, keep collaboration alive, support difficult decisions, struggle for consensus, strengthen emotional intelligence, negotiate differences, and resolve conflicts in ways that repair relationships and end in reconciliation.

5. *Linking Intention with Results: Skills in Committed Action:* Committed action requires democratic leaders to radically expand participation and available options, winnow them down through consensus, and design experiments or pilot projects if consensus fails.

Democracy, collaboration and mediation, above all, require a sharing of power. For them to become consistent and widespread, we need to become *owners*, and not merely renter of our lives and relationships. And who is going to design, build, own, and sustain these leadership skills? The only answer, in democracies, is *we* will, together.

A TRANSFORMATIONAL APPROACH TO CONFLICTS BETWEEN POLICE, DEMONSTRATORS, AND COMMUNITIES OF COLOR

Police everywhere receive extensive training in using rifles, pistols, tasers, and clubs. How much training do they receive in non-violent communication, de-escalation, collaborative negotiation, and mediation?

Every officer learns to use violence and the martial arts. How many learn empathy, compassion, and emotional intelligence?

Police in all communities are taught to recognize and respond to aggression, but how many are taught to recognize and respond to systemic racism or sexism? How many know how to express empathy, or when to refuse an order, or how to apologize or forgive? All are trained in the letter of the law, but how many understand its spirit, or its relationship to justice?

Throughout history, police have played mixed and complex roles. One has been to maintain "law and order," which has meant keeping Blacks and Browns, feminists, gays, organized labor, and all discriminated and oppressed people in their place — quiet, subordinate, and obedient to those who stand over and above them, by periodically applying a knee to their necks.

It is time to take a transformational, systemic approach to chronic conflicts between police, political demonstrators, and communities of color. What might this approach look like?

There have been numerous calls to abolish or defund police departments, but it is not entirely clear what this would entail, other than rebuilding, as in Camden, New Jersey. A *transformational* approach to policing would seek to:

- Strengthen non-violent communication, collaborative negotiation, and mediation skills, with a focus on prevention;
- End mass incarceration and imprisonment through house arrest and "pay for law-abiding' programs;
- Decriminalize sex work, addiction, homelessness, drug use, and consensual, victimless "crimes";
- Provide counseling, housing, guaranteed annual incomes, community-based drop-in centers, integrated assistance, and social and health services for those in need;
- Adopt a non-confrontational, constitutionally supportive approach to political demonstrators, rather than banning, blocking, beating, or tear-gassing them, which routinely *provokes* violence rather than preventing it;
- End the use of police to dominate and suppress those who object to being discriminated against and treated unfairly by protecting and taking the side of those who discriminate;
- Defund and dismantle the war culture and weaponry of police departments, which treats demonstrators and communities of color as the enemy, and support peace-building and de-escalation.

As mediators, dialogue facilitators and conflict resolution systems designers, we have had decades of experience addressing these issues in a variety of settings, and can propose options, based on these experiences. For example, here are ten:

1. That *all* police and community leaders be trained in non-violent communication, collaborative negotiation, public

dialogue facilitation, and restorative justice — and paid to mediate disputes, rather than assume that violence is the only method for solving problems

2. That police and cities publicly apologize for past incidents of racial discrimination, and for failing to listen to and negotiate with demonstrators and minority communities before resorting to unnecessary force, violence and coercion

3. That police and cities invite the public to participate in regular facilitated dialogues on police/community relations to discuss what has happened in the past and invite recommendations for change

4. That cities create multi-stakeholder "Blue Ribbon" commissions and on-going police review boards, and work with police unions to assess what has happened in police/community relations and why, and correct it;

5. That police and cities declare a policy of using violence only as a last resort, disarm patrol officers, and commit publicly to first and primary use of non-violent methods

6. That police and cities recognize the need to develop a completely different culture, approach, and attitude toward policing that is less confrontational and discriminatory toward communities of color, and more collaborative, humane, and egalitarian

7. That all cities establish, increase funding, and prioritize programs in restorative justice, victim/offender mediation, and community mediation

8. That all police teams include at least one "good cop" who has been extensively trained in mediation, negotiation, and the art of listening

9. That community mediation programs be funded to train police and other city departments in bias, prejudice, and stereotyping; and to build the skills and capacities of social justice organizations, community policing programs, police review boards, and neighborhood watch participants in conflict resolution, consensus building and problem solving

10. That cities initiate a conflict resolution systems design

process to identify the sources of chronic conflict involving
the police and criminal prosecution, and propose
alternatives, such as mediation, restorative justice,
sentencing circles, and Multi-Door Courthouses.

These are just a few ideas out of hundreds that might emerge from
police/community dialogues. What matters now is that we take
advantage of this opening to change and propose new ways of
extending egalitarian, democratic, *mediative* principles to the entire
system and culture of policing. To do so, we require sustained efforts
at improvement, the election of courageous political leaders from top
to bottom, and a determination to build the skills we all need to
build an authentic, substantive, engaged and humane democracy.

PLANTING SEEDS OF PEACE

CELEBRATING MEDIATORS BEYOND BORDERS

This chapter is transcribed from a speech I gave at Cardozo School of Law celebrating the anniversary of the founding of Mediators Beyond Borders, and published in the Cardozo Law Review.

We must come to see that the end we seek is a society at peace with itself, a society that can live with its conscience.

— MARTIN LUTHER KING JR.

[F]ear of feeling makes us inflict on one another the little murders of the soul that anesthetize the spirit and shrivel the heart; stifle desire and humiliate sentiment; make war electrifying and peace dreary.

— VIVIAN GORNICK

Don't do anything less than all you are capable of, and remember that history outlives you. It may not be until your grandchildren's days that they'll point back and say, there were sown the seeds of what we've now achieved.

— CAMILLA SHAMSIE

M ediators Beyond Borders began many years ago, as I was watching television coverage of the "shock and awe" bombing of Baghdad by the U.S. military. As I watched B-52 bombers flying over the city dropping bombs that could not help but reach civilian targets, my mediator's empathy for those on the ground became nearly overwhelming, and my brain responded with the fantasy that –, instead of bombs, out of the B-52's mediators would parachute by the tens of thousands, each with our little clipboards and pens. I smiled at the thought, but then began to think: what would we do when we hit the ground?

From this safe and tame fantasy emerged a far more wild and more dangerous one — that mediators could actually make a difference *globally*, by building conflict resolution skills and capacities in communities everywhere, and thereby help create "a more peaceable world."

I later came to realize that every conflict creates borders and walls that separate us into competing races, genders, religions, castes, and classes; that the problems we face are increasingly global and require collaborative global solutions; that mediation is always and everywhere a border-crossing methodology; and (to quote Angela Davis, "bridges are just walls that have been turned sideways."

At first, we simply wanted to be without borders, but then realized that we needed to move beyond them, and to find ways of inviting human hearts and heads to connect, collaborate, support one another in solving problems, and thereby turn all our differences into strengths.

We began with a request to assist a group of child soldiers at the Bududuram refugee camp in Ghana, which then extended to Liberia, and Kenya, and from there to Sierra Leone, Nigeria and Sudan. At the same time, we began working in the U.S. with Somali refugees, then with residents of the Ninth Ward in New Orleans after Hurricane Katrina. We organized an international team of mediators to attend the U. N. Climate Change conference in Copenhagen, and every U.N. climate change meeting afterwards, to advocate for mediation and conflict resolution over environmental issues. We helped train people from the U.N.'s Mediation Support Unit and Assistant Secretary General's office of Ombuds and Mediation Services, met with U.N. Women working for a better world, and trained women in different regions around the world in leadership, conflict resolution, and peace building. The list goes on and on, and in every one of these examples, we were the ONLY mediation organization in the world to do so. Would that there were hundreds.

Our work is not even *nearly* done. This celebration takes place in a moment of escalating political conflict around the world, and while many in our profession have regarded political conflicts as outside mediation, we do not have the luxury of continuing to do so. We *desperately* need to develop a new form of advocacy, an interest-based form of democracy, and new forms of mediation and dialogue that can respond successfully to political conflicts — and Mediators Beyond Borders is doing so, through its initiative, Democracy, Politics and Conflict Engagement (DPACE), its global webinars on the pandemic, its dialogues on racism and police conflicts, and similar efforts.

We continue planting seeds of peace and conflict resolution around the world, in hopes that they will someday bear fruit. I like to think of it this way: we can count the number of seeds in an orange, but we cannot count the number of oranges in a seed. That is the power of this work, and why this award is so important, and why it does not really belong to MBB, but to the countless people around the world we are working with who, faced with violence and poverty and repression, courageously strive every day to plant the seeds of peace and dispute resolution that someday will feed all our children. Thank you for supporting that. With deep gratitude and renewed dedication,

NEUTRALITY, OMNI-PARTIALITY, AND THE EVOLUTION OF POLITICAL CONFLICT

The hottest places in hell are reserved for those who in times of great moral crises maintain their neutrality.

— DANTE ALIGHIERI

Washing one's hands of the conflict between the powerful and the powerless means to side with the powerful, not to be neutral.

— PAULO FREIRE

If you are neutral in situations of injustice, you have chosen the side of the oppressor. If an elephant has its foot on the tail of a mouse and you say that you are neutral, the mouse will not appreciate your neutrality.

— DESMOND TUTU

E very conflict asks us to take sides, to add our weight and energy, our hearts and minds, bodies and brains, in support of one side over and against another. However, we respond, we help carve the riverbeds and shape the unseen channels through which our futures, and those of succeeding generations, will flow. We *create* ourselves, and the cultures, contexts, systems, and environments we will live in. We offer hope or withhold it. We open and shut our hearts.

Nowhere is this truer than in political conflicts, where our lives depend on the outcome of polarized contests that determine not only winners and losers, victors and vanquished, but the sort of world we will live in, the quality of life we will enjoy, and the possibility of success and happiness.

In response, mediators have refused to take sides, but this refusal can take two forms: first, neutrality, in which we distance ourselves from both sides and reject the zero-sum factual truths they espouse and advocate; or second, "omni-partiality," in which we place ourselves on *both* sides at the same time, and affirm the underlying emotional and "heart" truths they represent.

In 2001, in *Mediating Dangerously,* I suggested we shift our thinking from being neutral to being omni-partial, first, because there is no such thing as genuine neutrality when it comes to conflict; second, because the *language* of neutrality creates an expectation that fairness means suppressing our past experiences and insights:

> But real fairness comes from using the past to gain an open, honest, *humble* perspective on the present. Worse, neutral language is bland, consistent, predictable, and homogenous, and used to control what cannot be controlled.... Yet because neutrality implies objectivity and distance from the source of the conflict, it cannot countenance empathy, or give the mediator room to acknowledge or experience grief, compassion, love, anger, fear, or hope. Neutrality can paralyze emotional honesty, intimate communication, vulnerability, and self-criticism. It can undermine shared responsibility, prevention, creative problem solving, and organizational learning. It can ignore the larger systems in which conflict occurs. It can fail to comprehend spirit, forgiveness, transformation, or healing, which are essential in mediation. As a

result, it can become a straitjacket, a check on our ability to unlock the sources of conflict.

What is the meaning, for example, of neutrality, or compromise, in contests between dictatorship and democracy, war and peace, slavery and freedom, hate and love, cruelty and kindness?

Yet mediation teaches us that all conflicts contain multiple truths. These are not the simple, superficial, one-sided factual truths parties often argue over, but the deeper, more complex, multi-faceted emotional and heartfelt truths that *synthesize* their diverse perspectives, creating wholes that are greater than the sums of their parts.

Omni-partiality does not require us to agree or disagree about *facts*, but asks us to encourage empathy and dialogue over *meanings*; and to reject adversarial, competitive judgments grounded on distinctions between "us" and "them." It "separates the person from the problem," allowing us to be "soft on the person and hard on the problem," and inclusive of everyone, without collapsing multiple truths into some simplistic, superficial, one-sided façade of Truth. At the same time, it is grounded in core values, such as inclusion, diversity, respect, honesty, collaboration, and caring.

Isaiah Berlin believed that *all* politics, and by extension, all political conflicts, are *inherently* unscientific, because they are open, fluid, unpredictable, pluralistic, and changing; and therefore, according to Karl Popper's definition of science, they are *un-falsifiable*, as they concern a future that is undetermined and has yet to happen.

This suggests that scientific truths, like Covid-19 and global warming, are *not* themselves political, although our attitudes and responses to them may be. Neither neutrality nor omni-partiality make any sense in response to mathematical or scientific inquiries. On the other hand, what democracy, collaboration, and mediation all *uniquely* require, as interest-based processes, is inclusion, diversity, and a complex, omni-partial search for the deeper, multifaceted, *complementary* truths that unite us.

As an illustration, we can ask three *categories* of question in any group:

1. Who is the oldest or youngest, tallest or shortest person in the group? The outcome will be a single correct answer for everyone.
2. How old or tall are you? The outcome will be a single correct answer for each person.
3. What issues are you facing at your age? What does your height mean to you? The outcome will be multiple correct answers for each person.

Through these questions we can recognize an *evolution* in our approach to differences, applicable in political conflicts, that moves from power-, to rights-, to interest-based approaches, with higher *orders* of complexity, collaboration, and skill in language, process, and relationship required of each. Here, for example, are the same three orders with regard to the language of politics, its' sources and consequences:

1. *The Language of Power:* The language favored by power-based organizations such as the military, police, autocracies, and monarchical states requires clarity, simplicity, and uniform interpretation in order to encourage unthinking obedience. The communications that emanate from these institutions therefore take the form of declarations, pronouncements, and orders, which reinforce hierarchy and command, and imply punishment and contempt for those who disobey.
2. *The Language of Rights:* The language favored by rights-based organizations such as legal institutions, bureaucracies, and *procedurally* democratic states, requires narrow distinctions, exceptions, and adjudicated interpretations in order to maintain control by permitting some behaviors and forbidding others. The communications that emanate from these institutions take the form of rules and regulations, policies and procedures, legislative definitions, and legal

interpretations, which reinforce bureaucracy and control and imply coercion and censure for those who do not fit in.

3. *The Language of Interests:* The language favored by interest-based organizations such as teams, civil society, and *substantively* democratic states, requires affirmation of diversity, dissent, and dialogue in order to encourage collaboration and participation. The communications that emanate from these institutions take the form of open-ended questions, public dialogues, value-driven rules, and consensus decision making, which reinforce social equality, economic equity, and political democracy.

We can, on this basis, easily identify three alternative *interest*-based definitions of politics, each of which incorporates and encourages omni-partiality, (drawn from my book, *Politics, Dialogue, and the Evolution of Democracy*):

1. *Politics is a social problem-solving process.* As a result, a diversity of views about the nature of the problem and alternative ways of solving it will predictably result in better, more sustainable solutions.
2. *Politics is a large group decision-making process.* As a result, the greater the consensus, the stronger the democracy, and the more people agree with a decision the more likely it is to be effective.
3. *Politics is a conflict resolution process.* As a result, the amount of chronic, on-going, systemic conflict can be dramatically reduced by assuming there is more than one correct answer, and a complex, egalitarian, interest-based approach can result in no one having to lose so that that others are able to win.

Yet it sometimes happens in history, as William Butler Yeats wrote, that "the centre cannot hold," and adversarial politics "slouches" toward hatred, war, and authoritarianism. Why? One reason, I believe, is that history is asking us to choose between competing, increasingly divergent paths, as occurred in the U.S. over slavery as we approached the Civil War.

Another is that the conflicts we are facing can no longer be successfully resolved using lower order skills, and we need to invent or discover a higher order of attitudes and approaches, skills and techniques, that allow us to pool our resources and adopt methods of problem solving that are at least as rich, complex, and diverse as the problems they are intended to solve.

The social, economic, and political conflicts we face today, in my view, represent both. On the one hand, we are encountering a set of global problems that cannot be solved by individual nation-states using outmoded destructive, adversarial, and competitive methods that undermine international cooperation.

On the other hand, we increasingly need to evolve and develop higher order skills in the ways we respond — even locally — to Covid-19, racism, policing, global warming, and similar pressing issues, by optimizing our skills and capacity for inclusion, respect for diversity, collaboration, dialogue, democracy, non-violent communication, mediation, restorative justice, and similar interest-based processes.

Each of these crises asks us to overcome the hostile, adversarial, authoritarian forces that separate "us" from "them;" to realize that there *is* no "them," there is only us. And as we do, it becomes easy to be omni-partial, and on everyone's side at the same time, allowing us to face our conflicts and crises together, as a diverse and cohesive community of problem solvers.

8

MEDIATION, NEUTRALITY, POLITICAL CONFLICTS AND THE 2020 ELECTIONS

Of all the forms of inequality, injustice in health care is the most shocking and inhumane.

— MARTIN LUTHER KING, JR.

Even America feels today [1938] that democracy is not an assured possession, that it has enemies, that it is threatened from within and from without, that it has once more become a problem. [Politics] is no longer a game, played according to certain, generally acknowledged rules. … It is a matter of ultimate values.

— THOMAS MANN

The first lesson a disaster teaches is that everything is connected. In fact, disasters … are crash courses in those connections. At moments of immense change, we see with new clarity the systems – political, economic, social, ecological – in which we are immersed as they change around us. We see what's strong, what's weak, what's corrupt, what matters and what doesn't.

— REBECCA SOLNIT

I n the US, and in different ways in countries around the world, we are now facing five, and perhaps six significant crises, each with its own distinct set of conflicts:

1. *A Social Crisis*: Sparked by racism and police brutality, and extending to violence and discrimination against women, LGBTQ people, Jews, Muslims, Asians, immigrants, and others
2. *An Economic Crisis*: Sparked by the global lock-down, and extending to economic inequity, poverty, class exploitation, and prioritization of profits over people and planet
3. *A Political Crisis*: Sparked by autocracy and denials of the right to vote, and extending to gerrymandering, the Electoral College, voting by mail, and the continuation of democracy itself
4. *A Health Crisis*: Sparked by the Corona virus, and extending to Ebola and other diseases, the availability of health care for all, drug resistance, and attacks on science, disease experts, and the World Health Organization
5. *An Ecological and Environmental Crisis*: Sparked by global warming and species extinctions, and extending to air, water and soil pollution, destruction of rain forests and coral reefs, use of pesticides and fossil fuels, and ecological unsustainability

These seemingly separate and unique crises intermingle and interact, making all the others more serious and difficult to resolve without addressing them as well. They can therefore combine, amplify, and synergize, potentially giving rise to a sixth, multi-systemic *general* crisis, leading either to profound, far-reaching, transformational changes; or to regression, retreat, barbarism, and collapse.

Through these crises and conflicts, we are rapidly approaching a point on which the future of our planet, our people, our profession, and our personal lives, will pivot. The most immediate and important of these points will be reached in November 2020, with the election of a U.S. President and members of Congress (and therefore the Supreme Court), which will profoundly impact our global future.

The potential consequences can be seen in the extreme polarizations we are witnessing, just in response to Covid-19 and racism. On the one side are many Republican politicians, flanked by white-supremacist ultra-right militias armed with assault rifles, confederate flags, conspiracy theories, and Nazi regalia, demanding the lifting of health precautions, and harassing minorities and people wearing masks. On the other side are many Democratic politicians, flanked by healthcare professionals, grocery clerks, essential employees, and members of progressive and left political groups arguing for facts, science, personal protective equipment, and empathy, demanding equality and wearing masks.

These escalating polarizations extend to efforts to halt gender inequities, police violence, global warming, and climate change; to the advance of autocracy, hatred of foreigners, and the acceptability of pollution and environmental destruction; to the willingness to cooperate, or even participate in international partnerships; to the coercive use of military force, nuclear threats, protectionist tariffs, and denial of medical aid directed against "hostile" nations; to the continuation of explicit, implicit, and systemic bias, and intolerance of diversity; to the survival of independent journalism; to the right to vote; to whether political leaders are above the law; even to the *desirability* of democracy and constitutional government.

Polarization, in every conflict, is a sign that we are approaching a crossroads, a definitive choice, a point of departure. It is a signal that something deep, fundamental, and systemic has *already* been born; that the past is over, yet the future is uncertain and insecure; and that confusion, nostalgia, resistance, and fear of loss are intensifying in an effort to reverse course and return to a world that no longer exists, and *can* no longer exist.

What has any of this to do with the practice of mediation, peace building, and conflict resolution? Ultimately, *everything*.

As mediators, it is often difficult for us to assist those who are in conflict to listen to each other, communicate, engage in dialogue, jointly solve problems, collaboratively negotiate, and not just settle, but *resolve* their disputes. It is especially difficult to do so in deeply divisive, highly emotional, and immensely consequential political disputes, where there is resistance even to the *idea* of conversing, negotiating, or engaging in dialogue with "the other side," who are routinely stereotyped, demonized, and regarded with intense hostility and suspicion.

It is therefore *critical* that mediators, peace builders and conflict resolvers actively search for ways of plying these skills in political conflicts, and help turn divisive, excessively polarized conflicts in the direction of collaborative social problem solving, in part by designing, organizing, and facilitating democratic dialogues over difficult and dangerous issues.

Yet, it is essential in doing so, that we recognize the possibility that social, economic, political, health care, and environmental conditions can worsen and become so thoroughly polarized, and the parties so deeply discredited and reviled, that our efforts fail completely, making the work of communicating and connecting across even minimal differences nearly impossible —as often happens in active warfare, and under brutal autocracies and dictatorships.

In Nazi Germany, for example, what was actually, yet still somewhat invisibly at stake in the election of 1932, included the willingness to accept even the *existence* of Jews, communists, socialists, gypsies, homosexuals, people with disabilities, foreigners, "degenerate" artists, and other "undesirables," let alone to mediate, negotiate, or engage in dialogue and joint problem solving with them. In such times, as William Butler Yeats brilliantly described,

> *Things fall apart; the centre cannot hold;*
> *Mere anarchy is loosed upon the world,*
> *The blood-dimmed tide is loosed, and everywhere*
> *The ceremony of innocence is drowned;*
> *The best lack all conviction, while the worst*

Are full of passionate intensity ...
And what rough beast, its hour come round at last,
Slouches towards Bethlehem to be born?

In 1938, Hitler met in Munich with Mussolini, Chamberlain of Great Britain, and Daladier of France, ostensibly to prevent war and resolve conflicts over Czechoslovakia. Through several "collaborative negotiations" they reached a "mediated agreement" that resulted in the German takeover of Czechoslovakia, and convinced Hitler that the Allies would not risk war over the secretly planned invasion of Poland scheduled for the following year. Neither Czechoslovakia nor Poland, of course, were invited to the mediation, nor were any of those who would die in the ensuing conflagration. The mediator was Mussolini.

What happened in Munich is seen today as a classic case of betrayal, and what anthropologist Laura Nader, in her critique of mediation, called "trading justice for harmony." More deeply, it exposes a *political singularity*, a place of no return, both for democracy and mediation, foretold and set in motion by the election of 1932 and the polarizations fascism purposefully provoked in order to achieve these ends.

It is the intention of fascists everywhere to dominate and *annihilate* the Other; to deny the possibility of a common center that links us to one another; and to suppress and undermine all processes and methodologies that remind us of our common humanity and capacity for kindness – especially democracy, but also honest, principled, empathetic mediation and collaborative peace building. This is the "rough beast" whose face we can now make out not far in the distance, still somewhat isolated and disorganized, but growing in strength around the world and in the U.S., whose future we will vote on in November.

We will vote in November on the *idea* and the importance of social justice, economic equity, and political democracy. Additionally, we will vote on:

- Whether all citizens will have the right to vote
- Whether we will live in a democracy, and how authoritarian or participatory our political decision-making will be
- Whether the ruling party will be limited by the Constitution and the rule of law
- Whether the children of immigrants will be separated from their parents and held in prisons
- Whether we will listen to scientists and health care professionals in responding to pandemics
- Whether health care will be available to all
- Whether it will be regarded as acceptable anywhere in the world to attack or murder Blacks, Women, Jews, Muslims, and LGBTQ people
- Whether government officials and supporters of those in power will be investigated, prosecuted, and imprisoned for perjury, corruption and wrongdoing
- Whether we will partner with other nations in tackling world problems such as global warming, pollution of air, land and water, species extinction, environmental destruction, alternative energy, and similar issues
- Whether nuclear war anywhere in the world will be regarded as a legitimate option for resolving conflicts
- Whether we will continue supporting brutal dictatorships, the murdering and muzzling of journalists, and massive violations of human rights around the world — plus countless similar issues

It is especially important to understand that we will *also* be voting on the core principles and effectiveness of mediation; on the usefulness of dialogue, consensus building, collaborative negotiation, non-violent communication, appreciative inquiry, restorative justice, conflict coaching, and the continued growth and development of conflict resolution and peace building as a whole. Hostility to diversity and democracy always seek to expand beyond politics into workplaces and offices, art and social media, streets and public spaces, couples and families, and every conversation and conflict, undermining efforts to connect people everywhere.

As mediators, we are accustomed to finding or creating spaces for ourselves *between* opposing parties, and consider ourselves either "neutral," or as I prefer, "omni-partial," and on everyone's side at the same time. Yet here are five fundamental issues to keep in mind as mediators in designing public dialogues and seeking to resolve political conflicts:

1. It is important to understand that "neutrality" can mask bias and be complicit in preserving it. Desmond Tutu described it nicely: *"If you are neutral in situations of injustice, you have chosen the side of the oppressor. If an elephant has its foot on the tail of a mouse and you say that you are neutral, the mouse will not appreciate your neutrality."* Instead, we need to seek ways of *transcending* oppression, *both* for the oppressed and the oppressor, and thereby eliminate it as a source of chronic conflict.

2. It is important to distinguish advocacy for *positions* – i.e., for particular candidates, proposals, or solutions – from advocacy for *interests* —i.e., for democracy, mediation, dialogue, negotiation, peace building, inclusive processes, and collaborative relationships.

3. It is important to acknowledge, encourage, and support *everyone* in advocating and feeling passionately about their favored candidates, proposals, and solutions, and not seek to minimize their preferences or the strength of their convictions, but instead work to bring them into creative engagement, problem solving, dialogue, and constructive contention with one another based on their interests, commonalities, and the deeper meaning of their preferences or convictions. Inclusion, respect, empathy, and collaboration, whether in democracy, dialogue, or mediation, do not require *agreement* with either sides' logic, "facts," proposals, candidates, or content — but simply on a mutual

willingness to strive for fairness and respect in
communications, processes, and relationships.

4. It is important to recognize that democracy, like mediation,
   inherently requires systems, structures, processes, and
   relationships that are inclusive, diverse, egalitarian,
   equitable, and collaborative; that encourage and support
   joint problem solving, dialogue, consensus building,
   collaborative negotiation, and interest-based, rather than
   power- or rights-based communications; and that become far
   less effective when they are hierarchical, discriminatory,
   unequal, bureaucratic, adversarial, autocratic, or highly
   competitive.

5. It is important for us to learn how to adapt and apply
   conflict resolution processes and relationships to political
   disputes – not just for democratic values and principles to
   survive —but to encourage them to *evolve* and generate
   higher orders of communication, participation, collaboration,
   and engagement. Indeed, it is the *inability* to resolve
   intensely adversarial political disputes that impedes lower
   orders of democracy and conflict resolution, prevents them
   from evolving, and fuels the desire for authority figures and
   autocratic leaders to end conflicts by deciding for one side
   and against the other; nearly always by suppressing
   diversity and crushing dissent.

Most *procedural*, representative, indirect, bureaucratic, rights-based,
legally informed, *adversarial* forms of democracy discourage
independent group activity, permit only voting, and operate digitally
— for or against, either/or, with one party and against another, and
do not permit much popular input regarding content, process, or
relationships, or encourage transformational changes.

By contrast, *substantive*, participatory, direct, flexible, interest-based,
emotionally informed, *collaborative* forms of democracy invite
independent group activity, and operate analogically — us against it,
both/and, with all and against no one, and offer considerable voice

regarding content, process and relationship, and encourage transformational changes.

Because they require higher order, more complex, diverse, higher dimensional skills, they are able to solve higher order, more complex, diverse, and higher dimensional problems, which are increasingly essential to crack complicated and challenging global problems. I believe these higher order skills and capacities include, among others:

- An ability to work collaboratively, in partnership with diverse races, genders, cultures, classes, beliefs, personalities, physical conditions, and points of view
- A recognition of the value and importance of equality, caring, and authenticity in relationships, and a willingness to live them
- A willingness to explore and address implicit, systemic, and cognitive biases, and improve empathy and emotional intelligence
- A welcoming, curious, constructive attitude toward working with conflict, contradiction, ambiguity, enigma, and paradox
- An ability to acknowledge and affirm multiple truths, and to synthesize and creatively combine them in ways that reveal higher truths
- An ability to elicit personal stories, shameful narratives, painful experiences, unmet needs, and unsatisfied interests, and see them as requests for collaboration, mutual understanding, and change
- A willingness to search for ways of transforming fixed positions, beliefs, and ideas through artful questions, open dialogues, collaborative negotiations, emotionally intelligent conversations, and consensus building mediations

As mediators and conflict resolvers, we recognize the deep relationship, in all disputes, between diversity and collaboration, dialogue and empathy, democracy and respect, dignity and the right to participate in decision-making. We search for ways of inviting people in conflict to acknowledge and embrace each other; construct relationships based on equality and equity, community and caring; surrender the lopsided, polarized power- and rights-based privileges and adversarial attitudes that have divided us; and search together for interest-based solutions and common ground.

It is important, in doing so, to recognize that there are lower and higher forms of connection, cooperation, and common ground. The lower form can be found in compromise, which requires far fewer skills. If we ask, for example, "What common ground can we find between masters and slaves?" it is clear that *any* mediated compromise can lead only to more or less oppressive or expansive forms of enslavement — as occurred, for example, in the U. S. with the Missouri Compromise and the Compromise of 1850 — but not to its abolition. Finding lower common ground *implicitly* means siding with slavery and against slaves.

To reach higher common ground, it is necessary to affirm the common humanity of both parties, which implicitly requires not only the abolition of slavery, but reconstruction, elimination of bias, protracted dialogue, and a deeply honest, empathetic search for the human beings formerly known as masters and slaves. It is only through the use of higher order mediative, collaborative, democratic, dialogic, restorative justice processes that slavery, as a source of chronic, systemic conflicts, can not only be mitigated, but eliminated, transformed, transcended, and replaced by higher order, *human* conflicts.

In similar ways, elections in rights-based democracies are limited to lower order searches for *partisan* common ground, which routinely result in win/lose outcomes; chronic, unresolved, systemic conflicts; and compromises that may reduce harm or deescalate it, but rarely end, transform, or transcend it. As a result, we are periodically compelled by circumstances and fundamental principles to say and stand for what we believe in, and *then* to search for a higher common ground in which we abandon and exclude no one.

In crises, disasters, and intensely polarizing times, when neutrality and the center "cannot hold," the sources of chronic, systemic conflicts are revealed, and we can begin to see, as Rebecca Solnit describes, "what matters and what doesn't." It then becomes possible to transform fundamental values into higher order skills and capacities, processes and relationships, systems and structures, and extend empathy, cooperation, affection, and human decency to everyone everywhere.

Immediately following the November election, if a majority votes to reduce and resolve social, economic, political, healthcare, and environmental crises and conflicts, a broad range of collaboration, consensus building, dialogue, mediation, and conflict resolution skills will be needed, as those who lose will find it difficult to accept the outcome and may resort to violence; or refuse to mediate, engage in dialogue, or reconcile; or disrupt efforts to address the pandemic and other crises; or obstruct the ability to jointly invent and implement global solutions to the complex issues we face.

If, on the other hand, a majority votes to deny, ignore, suppress, or aggravate these crises and further polarize our conflicts, then democracy, mediation, and peace building will be pressured to retreat, water down their core values, become increasingly bureaucratic and superficial, and abandon their transformational promise — until people re-awaken, re-group, and realize what they have lost. Given the severity of the crises we face, these losses will be immense.

We therefore need to work hard for the candidates who will make it possible for mediation and dialogue to succeed, and vote for the kind of world we believe in and want to build. But if we want to transform our current crises and conflicts at their source, and create higher order substantive, diverse, collaborative, participatory, interest-based forms of democracy, we need to learn how to work together in higher order ways, using skills that do not undermine or contradict these core values. To do so, we will need mediators, collaborative negotiators, dialogue facilitators, consensus builders, conflict coaches, restorative justice practitioners, and peace builders of all kinds, willing to work in highly polarized neighborhoods and communities, workplaces and organizations, families and schools.

The time to strengthen our skills and capacity to both be and create the changes we want to see in the world is now. And we need to ask ourselves, with André Breton, "What are we waiting for? A woman? Two trees? Three flags? Nothing. What are we waiting for."

9

THE 2020 ELECTIONS, MEDIATION, AND THE POLITICAL DIVIDE — WHAT NEXT?

Our trust in the future has lost its innocence. We know now that anything can happen from one minute to the next. Politics, religion, economics, and the institutions of family and community all have become abruptly unsure.

— JOHN O'DONOHUE

> We had fed the heart on fantasies,
> The heart's grown brutal on the fare,
> More substance in our enmities
> Than in our love …

— WILLIAM BUTLER YEATS

Optimism is a strategy for making a better future. Because unless you believe that the future can be better, you are unlikely to step up and take responsibility for making it so.

— NOAM CHOMSKY

The scales of Justice weigh out gain
to those who've learned from pain ...

— AESCHYLUS

B iden and Harris won the election, but what *exactly* did they win? What was lost in the process? And, as mediators and citizens, what do we do next?

This was obviously an important victory for Democrats, but it has come at a significant cost for both democracy and dispute resolution. These costs can be seen in widespread refusals to accept the outcome, unwillingness to cooperate in transferring power, open support for the undemocratic principle of minority rule, armed threats to voting, opposition to even counting ballots, removal of polling stations in minority communities, intentional obstruction of the U.S. postal service, selective disenfranchisement of minority voters, bizarre gerrymandering, obstructive voter ID requirements, efforts to manipulate the Electoral College, knowingly false claims of electoral victory and voter fraud, and widespread efforts to undermine democratic principles. And all of it supported, at least tacitly, by a near majority of voters.

Over the last four years, we have witnessed a steady undermining of democratic rights and legal protections, and the creation and consolidation of an *infrastructure* and *scaffolding* that permit, excuse, and fan the flames of tyranny, despotism, autocracy, dictatorship, dishonesty, and yes, fascism. The fact that none of these were able to emerge full-blown in this election does not mean they could not have, or that they will not in some future election.

The perception that democracy and majority rule inevitably lead to the loss of power, wealth, and status by a previously dominant minority *inexorably* pushes their effort to regain dominance into ever more extreme, adversarial positions. Holding on to political power against the wishes of a majority *requires* the use of authoritarianism, demagoguery, hatred, lying, prejudice, militarism, moral corruption, bullying, environmental destruction, and dehumanizing violence.

These tools are needed to suppress democratic values, constitutional protections, civil rights, rule of law, and the freedoms of speech, assembly, religion, and the press – and with them, the possibility of political dialogue, collaborative negotiation, problem solving, consensus building, restorative justice, mediation, and the whole of conflict resolution. While these may seem like abstract and distant ideals, they impact the daily lives of all of us around the world.

These events are taking place in a *context* of chronic, unresolved national and international conflicts that deeply divide us, and threaten democracy both in the U.S. and abroad. These include conflicts over the economic impact and response to Covid-19 infections; nuclear threats and warlike "big stick" diplomacy against global competitors; openly prejudicial statements and hostility toward historically despised minorities; threats of violence and retaliation by armed ultra-right and neo-Nazi militias; growing poverty; and the expanding pace of global warming, environmental devastation, and species extinction – none of which have been adequately *acknowledged*, let alone discussed or addressed.

Each of these important and compelling issues takes the form of conflicts that *require* cross-cultural communication, joint problem solving, and collaboration between political adversaries; which, in turn, require higher order skills in non-violent communication, consensus building, dialogue facilitation, collaborative negotiation, impasse resolution, mediation, and similar interest-based processes. Yet these skills are nearly impossible to practice when the mere *idea* that there could be a middle ground is regarded as treasonous; when science is considered a conspiracy; and when dialogue, collaboration, and respect for legal rights are viewed as weaknesses that can legitimately be bypassed, outmaneuvered, or silenced though the use of force and violence.

As mediators, it is important to recognize that these losses and setbacks in the arena of politics are simultaneously losses and setbacks for the entire *project* of conflict resolution; for jointly tackling and solving our common problems; for democracy as a defense against bias, tyranny, and the silencing of political dissent;

and for resolving the complex social, economic, political, healthcare, and ecological conflicts and crises that increasingly threaten our global survival.

What, then, can we do? As a first step, we can acknowledge that addressing these issues requires, not just periodic elections and topical applications of political pressure, but a complete rethinking, redesign, and reorganization of political discourse, political decision-making, and the ways political conflicts are addressed and resolved.

If we view politics a *social problem solving,* and *conflict resolution* process, we can redesign it in ways that strengthen our ability to use collaborative, participatory, interest-based, consensus building, non-adversarial forms of political discourse and decision-making. This means acknowledging that complex, multi-faceted political issues concern alternative possible futures, and thus, *always* have more that one correct answer. Successful political problem solving therefore requires us to evolve beyond simplistic, one-sided, adversarial, winner-take-all processes and relationships; learn how to turn dissent and disagreement into improved outcomes; and remember that the richest and most important conversations always take place *beneath* the relatively superficial arguments people are having.

These insights suggest that we can use conflict resolution systems design principles to explore and implement a wide range of participatory methodologies and procedures, such as citizen's assemblies, focus groups, citizen's juries, town hall meetings, deliberative democracy, alternative forms of voting, community dialogues, sortation (used in ancient Athens), pubic policy and environmental mediation, large group consensus building processes, and similar efforts that broaden problem solving, deepen decision-making, and turn diversity in a less adversarial and more collaborative and democratic direction.

As a second step, we can strengthen our skills and capacities in using a rich, robust, and diverse array of processes, techniques, methods, and approaches to addressing political differences, such as reaching agreements on shared values, guiding principles, and ground rules;

asking questions that do not have a single correct answer; paradoxical forms of problem solving; creatively overcoming impasses; and using experimental approaches to implementation, such as pilot projects, charettes, rubrics, negotiated criteria, 360 degree evaluations, constructive feedback, and continuous improvement.

As a third step, we can recognize that political arguments, which seem hard-boiled, factual, and ideological on the surface, are actually deeply emotional, intimate, and heartfelt topics that have become over-heated and highly polarized, partly because they are framed as "either/or" alternatives that require one side to win and the other to lose; and partly because both sides care so deeply about issues that matter to them, and concern outcomes they care about.

Resolving political conflicts therefore requires *higher order* skills, not only in emotional intelligence, active and responsive listening, empathy building, non-violent communication, and appreciative inquiry; but in creative problem solving, group facilitation, conflict coaching, and opening heart-to-heart conversations between distrustful and passionate antagonists. While mediators and conflict resolvers practice these skills every day, we are not nearly as adept or skillful as we need to be in working with highly polarized political opponents.

What we have *not* yet done is figure out how to talk about these issues in ways that allow them to be resolved at a deeper level, and thereby become less divisive. The remedy is not to meet somehow in the "middle," for example, between slavery and freedom, or disenfranchisement and the right to vote, or dictatorship and democracy; but to see that these are manifestations of deeper, underlying dysfunctions in our conflict-promoting political systems, which unnecessarily position one person's gain as another person's loss, pitting us against each other, sometimes simply as a way of motivating voters to vote for otherwise lackluster candidates who promise to favor them over others.

The remedy is clear. It is to shift our political center of gravity from debates to dialogues, from bullying and epithets to open and honest communications, from closed-hearted to open-hearted conversations, from power- and rights- to interest-based forms of problem solving, from retributive to restorative justice, from lying and enduring enmity to truth and reconciliation.

The means, here, *are* the end, the process *is* the content, and the goal *is* the way we go about trying to achieve it. Our first challenge lies in learning how to coalesce into political *language*, into conversations, sentences, and words, a deep empathy for the person with a passionate commitment to solving the problem; an unconditional affirmation of respect and inclusion with an unconditional affirmation of dissent and difference of opinion; a desire for unity in facing problems with an acknowledgement of the value of diversity in our approaches to solving them, and willingness to disagree in pursuit of a deeper truth.

Here is a very small but powerful example of how to do this, revealed in what mediator Laura O'Neal wrote to her next-door neighbors before Election Day:

> Several of us have political signs in our yards. Me included. Some of you do not but may still have strong opinions about how this election should go. After this very heated and tumultuous election we are all still going to be right here. In our houses, on this block and in our community.
>
> When the votes come in there will be those of us who might be mad, feel slighted, or even despondent or might feel exuberant, relieved, happy.
>
> Regardless of how you voted, I want you to know that even though I feel very intensely about my choices and feel great concern about our country, I know that each family on this block is my country too. Just as I am multifaceted and not JUST my vote, the same is true for you.
>
> I care more about each of you than to put this election between us. It has taken me a long time to come to this. It feels like it has been a hot

mess, but somehow, I have gotten here. Perhaps we can have conversations after the election to find areas where we agree.

I challenge each of us to do one kind thing for someone on this block by the end of the year. It might be a smile, a batch of cookies or a homemade card of appreciation. You may not get a thank you. You may not get recognition, but I guarantee you will make a difference.

I'm glad to be a part of [our neighborhood].

There are countless opportunities for each of us to do something similar, in countless settings and situations. As the Sufi poet Rumi wrote,

Let the Beauty we love be what we do. There are hundreds of ways
to kneel and kiss the ground.

The law of entropy guarantees that there will always many more ways of undermining and destroying relationships than of building or advancing them, yet we have always progressed as a species more by working with, than against one another, and as our technological power and capacity for destructiveness continue to grow at an increasing pace, our challenge will be to strengthen communicative skills and capacity for collaboration at an equal or greater pace, if we are to avoid descending into barbarism and a war of each against all.

In conflicts and crises, our options ultimately boil down to two: go it alone, or face it together. We make these choices every day, as individuals, partners, and neighbors; but we also make them as organizations, societies, and nations. With the development of mediation, dialogue facilitation, collaborative negotiation, consensus building, and similar skills, we are now able to face our problems together and collaboratively solve them. All that is required is the decision, determination, and collective effort to make it happen.

10

50 QUESTIONS TO ASK IN POLITICAL ARGUMENTS

In the aftermath of the election, and as we head into the holidays when we will be talking with friends and relatives, we may find ourselves disagreeing with, in addition to the substantive points we want to make, here are 50 questions we can ask to help make our conversations more interesting and productive.

1. What life experiences have you had that have led you to feel so passionately about this issue?
2. Where do your beliefs come from? Family? Faith? Culture? Work?
3. What do you think your beliefs might be if you had been born into a different family, religion, race, gender, class, or time?
4. What is at the heart of this issue, for you as an individual?
5. Why do you care so much about this issue?
6. Do you see any gray areas in the issue we are discussing, or ideas you find it difficult to define?
7. Do you have any mixed feelings, doubts, uncertainties, or discomforts regarding this issue that you would be willing to share?

8. Is there any part of this issue that you are not 100% certain of or would be willing to discuss and talk about?

9. What questions or points of curiosity do you have for people who have different views?

10. What are some of the key words or phrases that divide us?

11. What are some of the key words or phrases that unite us?

12. What are some "hot button" political words or phrases for you?

13. How would you define each of those words or phrases? What do they mean, suggest, or imply to you? Why? What experiences have you had with them?

14. What emotions do you experience, or get triggered by, with each set of words?

15. Do you think other definitions, meanings, experiences, or emotions are possible? How?

16. What do you think our conversation would be like if we decided not to use the words that divide us or trigger us emotionally? Are you willing to try, right now?

17. Even though we hold widely differing views, are there any concerns or ideas you think we may have in common?

18. What underlying values or ethical beliefs have led you to your current political beliefs?

19. Do the differences between our positions reveal any riddles, paradoxes, contradictions, or enigmas regarding this issue?

20. What facts, if proven to be true, might cause you to think differently?

21. Is it possible to view our differences as two sides of the same coin? If so, what unites them? What is the coin?

22. Without discussing either of our preferred candidates, what principles do you believe the candidate you support stands for? Why are those principles important to you?

23. What are your goals for this election, other than to elect the candidate you support? Why are those goals important to you?

24. How might we extend those principles and goals to this conversation we are having right now?

25. What do these principles and goals require of us, in the way we treat each other, or how we talk to each other about the candidates we each support?
26. What forms of political argument or support do you feel are ineffective, counter-productive, or encourage you to resist?
27. What forms of political argument or support do you feel are effective, productive, or encourage you to think and learn from those you disagree with?
28. What ideals or principles do you think both candidates share?
29. What do you think will happen if our arguments or support become too adversarial or confrontational?
30. How might we work together to prevent that from happening?
31. Can you separate political issues from the people who hold them?
32. Is there anything positive or acknowledging you would be willing to say about the people on the other side of this issue?
33. Instead of focusing on the past, what would you like to see happen in the future? Why?
34. Do you think we are disagreeing about fundamental values, or over how to achieve them?
35. Is there any way that both of us could be right about different aspects of the issue? How?
36. What criteria could you use to decide which ideas or approaches work best?
37. What processes or ground rules could help us disagree more constructively?
38. Would it be possible to test our ideas in practice and see which work best? How might we do that?
39. What could be done to improve each of our ideas?
40. Could any of my ideas be incorporated into yours? How?
41. Is there any aspect of this issue that either of us have left out? Are there any other alternatives to what we are both saying?
42. What other information would be useful, or would you like

to have in order to address some of these questions we have discussed?

43. What could we do to improve our process for disagreeing with each other in the future? For encouraging future dialogue? Would you be willing to do that together?
44. Do you think this has been a useful and constructive conversation? If so, how? If not, what could we do better?
45. What is one thing I could do that would make this conversation work better for you?
46. Would you like to know one thing you could do that would make it work better for me? Are you willing to do that next time we talk?
47. What made you willing to participate in this conversation? Why did you agree to talk with me, even though we disagree?
48. What did you learn from our conversation?
49. What would you like to do differently in the future if we disagree? How could we make our dialogue ongoing or more effective?
50. Do you think it would be useful to continue this conversation, to learn more from each other and what we each believe to be true?

11

FROM DEMOCRACY TO FASCISM IN FIVE EASY STEPS, AND WHAT WE CAN DO TO STOP IT

I began writing this chapter in December 2020 and finished it on New Years Day 2021, in an effort to clarify the relationship between mediation, democracy, and fascism. The subsequent white supremacist "beer hall putsch" at the Capitol on January 6, 2021 has brought home how real the problem is and revealed the fragility and need for reform of our political system, as well as the true source of its democratic strength. While this attempted coup was, by comparison with other efforts, inept, ego-centered, half-hearted, and undisciplined, future efforts may not be so easily overcome, unless we take steps now to prevent them.

> [Fascist language] only serves the cause of invocation.... [It's] sole purpose ... is to strip everyone of their individuality, to paralyze them as personalities, to make them into unthinking and docile cattle in a herd driven and hounded in a particular direction, to turn them into atoms in a huge rolling block of stone.
>
> — VICTOR KLEMPERER

Every age has its own fascism. There are many ways of reaching this point, and not just through the terror of police intimidation, but by denying and distorting information, by undermining systems of justice, by paralyzing the education system, and by spreading in a myriad subtle ways nostalgia for a world where order reigned.

— PRIMO LEVI

Voice or no voice, the people can always be brought to the bidding of the leaders. That is easy. All you have to do is tell them they are being attacked, and denounce the peacemakers for lack of patriotism and exposing the country to danger. It works the same in any country.

— HERMANN GOERING

It is important to realize that he *could* have done it. The fact that he didn't, that he was too incompetent or self-centered or shortsighted to bring about the coup or putsch he has wanted and gravitated towards for years, does not mean he could not have succeeded, or that some future President who is more capable, determined, or willing, won't.

We can justly celebrate the survival of democracy and a successful electoral transition, but if we forget the last four years, or fail to explore how it could have, and still could happen here, and take steps to prevent that from occurring, we may not be as fortunate next time.

Only a few essential ingredients would be required to bring about a fascist dictatorship in the US. These include:

- A President who wishes to remain in power and is willing to undermine the electoral process in order to do so
- A critical mass of voters who are willing to support an autocratic leader, engage in "patriotic" violence and

intimidation, promote bias and bigotry, and suppress voting
by would-be opponents

- A majority of Senators who are willing to remain silent and
  do as they are told by the President
- Five members of the Supreme Court who are willing to
  affirm the emergency or war powers of the President, look
  the other way, and allow democracy to be bypassed

Once a demagogue has created unthinking loyalty in a near majority
of the electorate and substantial support in Congress and the courts,
the rest becomes relatively simple. Here are five easy steps to fascism
and effective dictatorship:

1. *Start a Reichstag Fire*: Without warning, the President could,
   for example, bomb Iran's nuclear facilities, destroy its air and
   naval forces, and selectively assassinate some of its top
   leaders, which would simultaneously create a state of war, a
   foreign enemy, a cycle of retaliation, internal "traitors," and
   justification for all the steps that follow.
2. *Declare Martial Law*: In anticipation of an Iranian counter-
   attack and terrorism directed at the US, the President could
   "temporarily" suspend elections and the rule of law, set
   aside the results of an election he claims was "stolen," and
   promise a new election to be conducted by the military at
   some unspecified time, after the crisis is over.
3. *Place Loyalists in Key Positions*: The President could appoint,
   for example, Michael Flynn as head of the Joint Chiefs of
   Staff, Rudy Giuliani as Attorney General, Steve Bannon as
   Chief of Staff, etc., tuning all aspects of government to a
   single key, coordinated by players willing to follow his
   orders, especially those that are illegal, immoral, and
   unconstitutional.
4. *Mobilize the Bullies and Thugs*: The President could call out the
   Proud Boys, MAGA supporters, White nationalists, and
   other groups on the far right, heavily arm, fund, and

discipline them, and direct them to terrorize the opposition. He could use war powers to order Homeland Security, ICE, and Customs and Border Patrol to arrest and imprison demonstrators and leaders of the political opposition, while delaying or temporarily suspending habeas corpus and legal appeals on grounds of martial law.

5. *Block the Distribution of Fake News*: Again using martial law and war powers, the President could suspend news operations at the New York Times, Washington Post, CNN, MSNBC, etc.; appoint a regulatory commission to suppress "fake news" and information that might provide "aid and comfort to the enemy," and arrest journalists who disobey.

Afterwards, other steps could be taken to consolidate power in the President, but these five are all that would be required to seize political power, push democracy to the side, cancel the results of a disappointing election, and instigate periodic threats to justify suspension of the Constitution, democracy, and the rule of law.

And to be clear, there is considerable, widespread, *open* support, even now, in January 2021, for all five of these steps among millions of voters.

This plausible scenario raises three obvious and compelling questions: first, if it is so simple, why didn't it happen? Second, what exactly is fascism, and what is required for it to be successful? And third, what can we do to stop it?

Why Didn't It Happen?

It is difficult to answer this question, as considerable effort over several years has gone into putting into place the infrastructural elements and pieces that support each of these steps, from provocative selective assassinations of Iranian officials, to "stand back and stand by" directives to Proud Boy supporters, to shocking descriptions of the press as "the enemy," and a litany of refusals to accept or be bound, even by hitherto unquestioned legal and Constitutional guarantees.

Fortunately, Iran saw through the ruse, realized it was being provoked into retaliation to justify a massive bombing campaign, and did not respond in kind. Instead of a military "October Surprise," there was Hunter Biden's computer, and again, a majority of the press saw through the ruse and did not take the bait. Similarly, a majority of the electorate saw through the falsehoods and biases, and instead of caving in, came out in unprecedented numbers to vote for a candidate who could not match the incumbent in charisma or clarity, but defeated him with the less popular qualities of decency and acceptance of science and facts.

Some of the failure of fascism is due, perhaps, to the fact that we are not living in a period like the 1930's in Europe, with social collapse, economic depression, defeat in war, and a real possibility of revolution. Some may also be due to the success of civil rights, feminist, and LGBTQ movements in de-legitimizing overt bias and raising awareness of its subtler, covert, and systemic expressions.

In addition, its principal proponents, starting with the President, simply took too long, losing allies with every delay; were not ruthless enough; did not succeed in completely crushing the opposition; and did not place in positions of power those who were prepared to act illegally and against the Constitution, but settled for minor players who were willing to loyally obey, undermine the institutions they headed, and lie in public, but not to take the final step into dictatorship.

Several deeper reasons fascism did not succeed in consolidating its control over the political process can be found in its' all-too-obvious incompetence and over-simplicity in addressing complex problems, like Covid-19; its political immaturity, false bravado, caginess, and ignorance of the nature of fascism itself.

What Is Fascism?

In *How Fascism Works: The Politics of Us and Them*, Jason Stanley, usefully outlines ten primary characteristics, dynamics, or features of fascism, each of which suggests the elements needed to make it successful, and the strategies and techniques that can be adopted to minimize, counter, and hopefully prevent it. Here is Stanley's list of characteristics, to which I have added a brief summary of what each aspect seeks to accomplish, drawn in part from Stanley's descriptions:

1. **Glorification of a Mythic Past:** Fascism seeks to instill pride, not with, but over and against others, and encourage loyalty, obedience, and sacrifice based on a version of the past that is heroic, arch-patriotic, unquestioning, propagandistic, and entirely imaginary.
2. **Propaganda:** Fascism seeks to distort, undermine, and prevent people from developing an accurate understanding of events, and encourage acceptance of illogical, irrational, and immoral acts through "alternative facts" and repeated assertion of simple formulaic falsehoods.
3. **Anti-intellectualism:** Fascism seeks to undermine science, crush dissent, and reinforce conformity in ideas and opinions by turning popular anger against elites and intellectuals, reducing opportunities for quality education, and offering overly simplistic, selfish solutions to complex problems that require collaborative efforts.
4. **Unreality:** Fascism seeks to promote distrust, fear, and anger, regardless of reality or circumstances, and replace the pursuit of truth with obedience to the self-serving, propagandistic views of those in power, partly by advancing bizarre, unreal, conspiratorial ideas, and rewarding loyalty, as measured by the willingness to affirm obvious falsehoods.
5. **Hierarchy:** Fascism seeks to support the domination of those with power, wealth, and status over those without, and to legitimize the discriminatory, oppressive, and inhumane treatment of others by imposing hierarchies and pecking orders in all areas of life.
6. **Victimhood:** Fascism seeks to justify its oppression and victimization of others by reversing reality and claiming to be their victims, thereby justifying and "reverse-

engineering" its own retaliation and cruelty to others, and revealing all its accusations to be confessions in disguise.

7. **Law and Order:** Fascism seeks to rationalize repression, dictatorial rule, and rejection of the principle that no one is above the law by forcefully imposing discipline, disguised as "law and order," in response to challenges, portrayed as "anarchists" or "socialists," who are defined as anyone who opposes, disagrees, or does not unquestioningly and fully obey.

8. **Sexual Anxiety:** Fascism seeks to promote sexual obedience, domination, and conformity as means of maintaining gender-based power and control, by encouraging fear of sexual "deviance," female independence, the sexual allure of minorities, and gender ambiguity and complexity.

9. **Sodom and Gomorrah:** Fascism seeks to undermine culture, art, and the diverse cosmopolitan values of cities by posing as traditional Biblical pastoral moralists, and railing publicly against "decadence," "perversion," and "amorality," while privately promoting them.

10. *Arbeit Macht Frei (Work Sets You Free):* Fascism seeks to glorify hard work, maximize exploitation and oppression, and turn laborers into willing, obedient robots, while consistently destroying labor unions, undermining class and caste unity, and removing all limitations on worker's health and safety, minimum pay, and bargaining power.

It is clear from this list that one of the core features of fascism is its' 180 degree reversal of the truth of whatever it claims. If it claims that work sets you free," in reality, it is doing what it can to ensure that work enslaves you. If it claims to be victimized, it is justifying and preparing to victimize others. If it claims others are stealing an election, it is intending to do so itself.

These reversals suggest still deeper transmutations of reality, in which pride acts as a mask for shame; rage appears as a masquerade and cover for fear; and bias against others surfaces as a substitute for self-loathing, fear of differences, loss of connection, and suppressed guilt and remorse. These distortions and substitutions allow the fascist experience of violence and victimization to be partially overcome – not by experiencing suffering oneself, or transforming it into empathy, kindness, and problem solving — but by becoming violent, falsely regarding it as patriotic and a strength, and using it to victimize others.

To understand fascism's intense emotional appeal and the fanaticism it inspires in its followers, it is essential to recognize the *torque*, tension, and energy that are generated in its' followers by twisting and compressing complex, higher dimensional, painful personal truths into simplistic, lower dimensional, aggressive political hostilities and prejudices against others.

Additional Definitions of Fascism

In *The Anatomy of Fascism*, Robert Paxton describes what he calls its "mobilizing passions," which include (with some edits):

- A sense of overwhelming crisis beyond the reach of traditional solutions
- The primacy of race and nation, toward which one has duties superior to every right, whether individual or universal, and the subordination of the individual to them
- The belief that one's group is a victim, a sentiment that justifies any action, without legal or moral limits, against its enemies, both internal and external
- Dread of the group's decline under the corrosive effects of individualistic liberalism, class conflict, and alien influences
- The need for closer integration of a purer community, by consent if possible, or exclusionary violence if necessary
- The need for authority by natural leaders (always male), culminating in a national chief who alone is capable of incarnating the group's destiny
- The superiority of the leader's instincts over abstract, scientific, logical, and universal reason

- The beauty of violence and the efficacy of will, when they are devoted to the group's success
- The right to dominate others without restraint from any kind of human or divine law, with the sole criterion being the group's prowess and success in a Darwinian struggle for survival

Many people have written extensively about fascism from many different perspectives in thousands of volumes, describing its political, economic, and social aspects throughout history. From these observations, we can identify more of its main features. In addition to large-scale definitions of fascism, we can identify others that capture its personal and social character, and lead us to consider more carefully what it looks like at the level of individual behavior.

The definitions of fascism that follow (many of which are mine, while others are based on writings by Erich Fromm, Umberto Eco, Wilhelm Reich, Hannah Arendt, Robert Paxton, Lawrence Britt, and others), present it not as the exclusive product of Germany, Italy, and Spain; or the genocidal policies of Hitler, Mussolini, and Franco; but as a *tendency* that arises in all nations and communities, and inside each of us, that we manifest in small ways every day. Here are a few aspects, elements, or definitions of fascism that point to solutions:

- Any set of beliefs, attitudes or behaviors that endorse the natural superiority of one race, gender, nation, religion, culture, group, or individual over others
- Hostility toward women as a group, as expressed through beliefs, attitudes, and behaviors that support their exclusion, male superiority, rape, and repression of sexuality; or justify sexual violence, brutality, harassment, and humiliation
- Forging alliances and "negative communities" based on fear of differences or hatred of others, especially Jews, people of color, ethnic and religious minorities, Roma, LGBTQ people, and those on the political left
- Homoeroticism combined with homophobia

- Enforced obedience, loyalty, and elitist submission to one's superiors, while regarding one's inferiors with contempt
- Encouraging, taking delight in, or refusing to apologize for brutality or cruelty; encouraging hatred; rejecting mediation and honest negotiation, and escalating conflict for the sake of conflict
- Identifying dissent and non-cooperation as disloyalty and treason
- Silencing opposition through intimidation and fear
- Using patriotism as a club to seize the status, wealth, or power of others
- Substituting external command for internal responsibility, and discipline by authority figures for self-discipline
- Appealing to the anger and violent instincts of frightened, frustrated, and humiliated people, while playing the role of their protector and master
- Taking pleasure in punishment and punishing pleasure
- Responding to failure by shaming and blaming others, and using demonizing and scapegoating as a substitute for self-criticism
- Adopting a simplistic, sloganistic, shaming vocabulary as a way of suppressing complex or critical thought
- Rejecting paradox, enigma, duality, ambiguity, and contradiction as descriptions of the nature of the world
- Wanting to "escape from freedom" through silence, conformity, and obedience to power
- Creating a cult of pride and glory in old traditions based on partial, ahistorical truths, and suppressing the criticism of historical events
- Promoting irrational, posturing, covert, and brutal action, while opposing reason, intellect, empathy, openness, and dialogue
- The worship of hierarchy and power, the dictatorship of the envious, the revenge of the weak
- The instrumentalization of truth, regarding it only a means of gaining or consolidating power

- The populism of those who want to be rich, and the unscrupulous rich who manipulate them
- The fear that democracy, elections, and majority rule will lead to socialism, and a transfer of status, wealth, and power from the rich to the poor
- Rejection of democracy and self-government as obstacles to self-aggrandizement
- Being obsessed with conspiracies and plots as explanations for loss, defeats, and powerlessness
- Bullying, humiliation, and domination over those who are seen as "weak," creating shame, guilt, fear of retaliation, and a divided self
- Creating a cult of heroism and death, or seeing life as warfare leading to inevitable Armageddon
- Wielding power as though it were the private property of an elite
- The suppression of art, together with the art of suppression
- Making evil appear banal, acceptable, legitimate, and ordinary
- Wanton exploitation of nature and destruction of the environment
- The simplification of language to the point that complex thought becomes impossible

What is essential in each of these elements is the recognition that fascism does not exist simply on a large scale, at the level of national political systems, but also on smaller scales, within and between us, and in the family, school, workplace, and community relationships we shape and participate in every day.

In this sense, fascism can be defined as the large-scale organization of small-scale hatreds; or on a personal level, as a failure of empathy, and an inability to find the Other within the Self. It is an *invitation* into enmity, distancing, and hatred, similar to the kind we experience on a small scale in ordinary, everyday conflicts, in which we routinely stereotype and dehumanize our opponents, disregard their issues and concerns, and seek to dominate and control what happens.

Many of these definitions require solutions that are not only national, political, and ideological, but operate on a personal, emotional, and behavioral level as well; solutions that can work in political and governmental arenas, and those that can be implemented by each of us in our personal relationships and everyday encounters, and in the attitudes and skills we bring to our conflicts.

Fascism as a Three-Part Process

These definitions of fascism, for all their richness, do not fully capture an important element that is essential to its long-term success. This is the element of acquiescence, complicity, condonation, or what became known in Europe during World War II as "collaboration." Historically, fascism has succeeded through a three-part process:

1. A top-down dismantling of democratic rights, practices, and institutions, largely by autocratic leaders
2. A bottom-up suppression of diversity and silencing of dissent, largely by armed groups of supporters
3. An individual and collective willingness to accept dictatorship, tolerate the dehumanization of others, capitulate to violence, remain silent, be obedient, and permit the gutting of democracy, largely by those who are angry at how they have been treated; or frightened, and simply want to survive, or escape being punished, or singled out for similar treatment

These elements create a clear, historic dividing line, amplifying differences between competing sides, and turning ordinary, everyday conflicts between opposing parties within a single society into conflicts between opposing *societies*; into *social* conflicts that assume an implacable, irreconcilable, political form.

Fascism comes to power not just by government leaders declaring martial law, asserting dictatorial powers, and launching political *coups d'etat*; but by their supporters threatening or instigating violence, and others capitulating to it; by some people speaking and acting in racist, sexist, and hateful ways, and others pulling back, retreating from empathy and solidarity, and tacitly accepting it; by some sparking conflicts or fanning their flames, and others surrendering, compromising, or blaming "both sides" for the problem.

This third element is aided by the attempts of professional politicians and elitist, top-down, "representative" forms of democracy to actively discourage popular participation in political decision-making, other than by selecting from a limited set of pre-framed alternatives that end in voting for or against, either/or, this candidate or that, this party or that, with few opportunities to openly and publicly discuss these options, or imagine, jointly design, and implement others.

Political professionals and elites are frightened of genuine citizen participation in politics, and confuse "populism," which rejects dialogue and diversity, and seeks safety and certainty in authoritarianism; with participatory forms of democracy, which encourage dialogue and diversity, and seek the more complex and creative uncertainty of direct engagement in democratic decision-making.

Three Forms of Democracy

Drawing from conflict resolution theory, we can identify three fundamental forms of democracy, corresponding to three principal approaches to problem solving, negotiation, and conflict resolution:

1. *Power-based, or repressive democracies*, in which only certain people are able to vote, often by affirmation, counting is corrupt, and candidates are limited to those acceptable to ruling elites, who dominate the process by virtue of their superior status, wealth, and power in win/lose, zero-sum,

rubber-stamp, internal power contests that are tightly controlled, repressive, encircled by violence, and completely behind closed doors

2. *Rights-based, or representative democracies*, in which voting for representatives is moderately restricted, governed by legal standards that are ostensibly neutral and independent of existing hierarchies, yet in fact are controlled by them, also in limited, win/lose, zero-sum, exercises of rights that are indirectly manipulated through campaign contributions by wealthy donors, controlled by courts and political elites, and take place superficially in public, but substantively in private

3. *Interest-based, or participatory democracies*, in which discussions and voting are on substantive issues and nearly universal, with direct participation through facilitated political dialogues, consensus building, joint problem solving, collaborative negotiation, mediation, and similar methods, resulting in win/win, mutual gain, satisfactions of interests, that are inclusive, jointly designed, open to change, participatory, and public

Over time, we can observe a gradual evolution from power- to rights- to interest-based forms of political decision-making, primarily as a result of the increasing complexity and global nature of problems we are required to solve, and a growing need for communication and collaboration across power- and right-based borders, walls, and separations, with all their inequalities, inequities, and chronic hostilities, in order to successfully overcome and resolve them.

Most importantly, if fascism succeeds through a *combination* of violence and capitulation, of conflict and acquiescence, preventing it will require solutions that are able to halt, de-escalate, and prevent violence; that draw people into dialogue and empathetic connection with one another; that support democratic processes; and that build the capacity to settle and resolve conflicts through nonviolent, non-adversarial, interest-based processes and relationships.

What Can We Do to Stop It?

As a result of these very different definitions and understandings of fascism, we can see that joint problem solving, consensus building, open and honest communication, empathetic listening, prejudice reduction, bias awareness, collaboration, community building, interest-based bargaining, dialogue facilitation, mediation, peace building, and conflict resolution practices generally, can contribute significantly to reducing the strength and sway of fascistic thinking, both on small and large scales.

If the primary purpose of fascism is to preserve or reinstate historic hierarchies of status, wealth, and power by defending the practice of domination and innate superiority – be it of a person, class, caste, race, gender, religion, nation, culture, etc., then the logical, essential, and compelling response ought to be to strengthen interest-based democratic processes, relationships, and systems; to reduce rigid and imposed hierarchies; to encourage the sharing of status, wealth, and power; and to invite widespread, direct participation in social, economic, and political dialogue and decision-making, starting with those who have been most frequently and thoroughly excluded.

More deeply, if the central purpose of fascism is to divide and pit us against one another, to separate "us" from "them" in order to reinforce hierarchies of domination and superiority on all levels; if it is to use authoritarianism, intimidation, and violence to hoard status, wealth, and power and take them from others, it would make sense for those who oppose fascism not merely to promote social equality, economic equity, and political democracy, and extend empathy, kindness, and generosity to those who have been castigated, stereotyped, oppressed, and excluded; but in the process of doing so, to also:

1. Redesign electoral processes to reduce opportunities for demagoguery, graft, dishonesty, and corruption; guarantee one person/one vote; and reduce resort to violence and viciousness, partly by means of citizen's assemblies, focus groups, citizen's juries, town hall meetings, deliberative

democracy, alternative forms of voting, sortition, community dialogues, public policy and environmental mediations, facilitated large group consensus building, and joint problem-solving processes, etc.

2. Redesign, reconfigure, and reprioritize the work of institutions that engage in, promote, and encourage violence, such as police and military forces, through expanded training, prioritized funding, and rewarding efforts at de-escalation, non-violent communication, problem solving, hostage-style negotiation, mediation, restorative justice, community policing, review boards, and similar methods, as first responses to conflict

3. Dramatically expand, strengthen, institutionalize, and increase funding for collaborative, participative, mediative, and other interest-based social, economic, and political processes, including widespread, coordinated dialogues regarding difficult and divisive issues, empathy building circles, transnational environmental mediation, community problem solving, and conflict resolution systems design

Fascism *invites* its opponents to fight back, and welcomes their responsive hatred and violence, which allow it to sustain its stereotypes, backwards justify its actions, and impose the kind of contest in which it is likely to be successful. Yet, as Martin Luther King, Jr. eloquently wrote, based on a lifetime of experiences,

> The ultimate weakness of violence is that it is a descending spiral, begetting the very thing it seeks to destroy. Instead of diminishing evil, it multiplies it ... Through violence you may murder the liar, but you cannot murder the lie, nor establish the truth. Through violence you may murder the hater, but you do not murder hate. In fact, violence merely increases hate ... Returning violence for violence multiplies violence, adding deeper darkness to a night already devoid of stars. Darkness cannot drive out darkness; only light can do that. Hate cannot drive out hate; only love can do that.

Ultimately, it is our unwillingness to surrender our humanity, even in the face of violence and inhumanity; our openness to communication, even with those who despise and will not speak to us; our commitment to include in democracy even those who would destroy it; and our courage to face and fix what isn't working within it, that will allow us to design a more evolved, inclusive, and successful democracy, and avoid the ominous fate we have been privileged to foresee.

12

10 ACTIONS WE CAN TAKE TO TURN ADVERSARIAL, AUTOCRATIC, POWER-BASED POLITICAL CONFLICTS INTO COLLABORATIVE, DEMOCRATIC, INTEREST-BASED SOCIAL PROBLEM SOLVING

I wrote this article on January 7, 2021, to suggest a few specific, practical, small-scale, local ways mediators can strengthen democracy and help it evolve in an interest-based direction, consistent with mediation values, and without requiring any deep understanding of fascism. I hope you enjoy them both and find them useful.

We have taken democracy for granted and allowed it to be undermined and chipped away by elected officials, for whom it is only a means of gaining status, wealth, and power. And we have come within a hair's breadth of losing it.

Imagine, for example, where we might be today if a mere handful of disciplined, heavily armed white supremacists had held Congress hostage, "arrested" a few recalcitrants, and blocked them from certifying the votes of the Electoral College; or if Trump had personally, as promised, led them into Congress; or if, as advised, he had ordered the arrest of Pence, Biden, Harris, and a few others, canceled the election as fraudulent, and declared martial law.

Because democracy is open, it is vulnerable to demagogues and autocrats; yet because it is open, it is also resilient, able to learn and improve, and responsive to popular wisdom. In order to avoid similar occurrences in the future, it now needs to evolve — especially in its responses to conflict, and its ability to welcome diversity and dissent.

Key to doing so, is its' ability to turn adversarial, autocratic, win/lose, power- or rights-based political processes that automatically trigger political conflicts, into collaborative, democratic, win/win, interest-based ones that transform political conflicts into social problem solving.

The "whys" of doing so are now obvious; it is the "hows" we need to address. We can begin simply, and locally, with ten steps every aspiring mediator can take, starting with these:

1. Strengthen our skills and receive training in the full range of conflict resolution methods, including diverse forms of mediation, as well as dialogue and circle facilitation, consensus building, informal problem solving, collaborative negotiation, nonviolent communication, appreciative inquiry, restorative justice, and especially large group, multi-stakeholder, organizational, environmental, and public policy mediations, and conflict resolution systems design.

2. Join and become active in organizations that are working to shift political discourse, spark democratic dialogues, discuss difficult and dangerous issues, or influence political leadership — organizations like Essential Partners, Living Room Conversations, Better Angels, National Coalition for Dialogue and Democracy, Karuna Center for Peacebuilding, Days of Dialogue, Everyday Democracy, Mediators Beyond Borders International (MBBI), and its initiative, Democracy Politics and Conflict Engagement (DPACE), and many others.

3. Email, call, or personally contact local city and county officials, including city managers, housing and planning departments, and offer to facilitate conflicted public meetings, mediate local political conflicts, or design a

consensus building process, for example, to come up with solutions to homelessness.

4. Reach out to local activists and political organizations, like Black Lives Matter, Indivisible, Greenpeace, and others of all persuasions, and offer assistance in facilitating meetings and resolving internal conflicts; or make presentations, conduct trainings in conflict resolution, or observe and mediate at demonstrations or coalition meetings with other groups.

5. Contact local law enforcement, including police and sheriffs departments, and offer to conduct quick morning briefings for officers on practical de-escalation, active listening, emotional calming, and mediation techniques; or to facilitate community meetings to discuss, for example, ways of prioritizing funding to reward efforts at de-escalation, non-violent communication, problem solving, hostage-style negotiations, mediation, and restorative justice; or to discuss community policing, review boards, and similar methods, as first responses to conflict.

6. Write articles, op-ed pieces, and letters to local and national newspapers and on social media, critiquing politically biased, adversarial, and propagandistic forms of political rhetoric from a conflict resolution perspective.

7. Start or support local school and community mediation programs; or volunteer to help train students, parents, teachers, and administrators in peer mediation; or offer to speak to leaders of civic and community organizations in conflict resolution approaches and techniques.

8. Contact local political leaders, elected officials, and political party representatives, and offer to facilitate meetings to redesign electoral processes so as to reduce opportunities for demagoguery, graft, dishonesty, and corruption; guarantee one person / one vote; reduce resort to violence and viciousness; and increase trust in election outcomes.

9. With city and county officials and community organizations, explore the local use of facilitated public planning, brainstorming, problem solving, and democratic decision-

making practices, such as town hall meetings, citizen's assemblies, focus groups, community dialogues, citizen's juries, deliberative democracy, alternative forms of voting, sortition, public policy and environmental mediations, community-wide strategic planning, facilitated large group consensus building sessions, informal creative problem solving conversations, and similar processes.

10. Ask to appear before local city councils and boards of supervisors to support expanding, strengthening, institutionalizing, and increasing funding for collaborative, participative, mediative, and other interest-based processes, and encourage the sponsoring of widespread local community dialogues regarding difficult and divisive political issues, or empathy building circles, or community mediation programs, and of designing free, comprehensive, integrated conflict resolution systems at all levels of government.

None of these alone will be sufficient by themselves, yet each contains, in miniature, a core idea that can be scaled-up to higher levels, expanded, and supported in broader applications. None of these is beyond the ability of mediators, or outside our expertise, and none requires us to take sides on the substantive political issues over which people disagree, except in so far as our professional experience supports the values of diversity and equality.

Conflict resolution is an idea whose time has come, yet it is clear that implementing it will not be easy, quick, or without challenges. Shifting from adversarial, autocratic, power-based political conflicts requires a critical mass of local leaders, officials, and infrastructures with experience in collaborative, democratic, interest-based social problem solving. These, in turn, require higher order skills on our part. Developing and applying these skills and making these ideas real is up to us, because there is no one else who can deliver them.

None of these ideas or programs presently exist, except in miniature, in small pockets, and in the hopes and hearts and minds of millions, who *know* it is possible. They live also in us, because we have *done* them countless times, over and over, and daily for decades — with couples and families, schools and communities, litigators and adversaries, even warring parties, and we *know* that they work. All that is required now is for us to step up and prove it. The world is watching, hoping, and waiting.

13

INSURRECTION, DEMAGOGUERY, AND THE MEDIATION OF POLITICAL CONFLICTS

[Partisan demagoguery] agitates the community with ill-founded jealousies and false alarms, kindles the animosity of one part against another, foments occasionally riot and insurrection. It opens the door to foreign influence and corruption, which finds a facilitated access to the government itself through the channels of party passions.

— GEORGE WASHINGTON

Elections belong to the people. It's their decision. If they decide to turn their backs to the fire and burn their behinds, then they will just have to sit on their blisters.

— ABRAHAM LINCOLN

[T]he law is not an instrument to find out the truth. It is there to create a fiction that will help us move past atrocious acts and face our future. It seems there is no mercy in this world, but a kind of haphazard justice: men pay for crimes, but not necessarily their own.

— HILARY MANTEL

F ollowing the "insurrection," "putsch," or "attempted coup" in Washington D.C., on January 6, 2021, and the subsequent acquittal of President Trump on impeachment charges, we find ourselves facing extremely significant and difficult, yet very different political conflicts and challenges from those we faced before.

Because the attempted takeover of the U. S. government was *not* successful, but could have been; because the threat it represents is on-going and likely to recur; because it stimulated intense political passions and reinforced the use of deeply flawed, emotionally charged language to describe political opponents who are also fellow citizens; because it went to the heart of our moral, social, economic, and political character; and because it substantially weakened the core principles of our democracy, it is essential that we not just "forgive and forget," and swiftly move on to more immediate concerns, but stop for a moment and consider carefully *how* we should respond, and what, if anything, our experience as mediators resolving adversarial disputes in diverse settings over several decades can teach us about how we might de-escalate, settle, resolve, and prevent highly polarized political conflicts.

These events reveal, on the one hand, how fragile our democracy is; and on the other, how potentially robust it is – and how important it is for us to find less adversarial and more collaborative methods for resolving political disputes. It is important for us to understand the costs of escalating rhetoric and false polarization, and learn how to talk – not *at*, or even *to*, but *with* each other; and to listen – not superficially or defensively, or only to insults and falsehoods, but empathetically and collaboratively, to commonalities, perceptions, feelings, life experiences, passions, and a broad range of subtle, complex, paradoxical truths that underlie our political conflicts — and to do so *without* asking people to sacrifice, abandon, or devalue their values or understandings of the world, their attitudes toward themselves and others; or their passionately held principles and beliefs.

To begin, it is important that we recognize the rapid growth of white supremacist, neo-fascist, conspiratorial hate groups in the US, and that they nearly succeeded in overturning democracy, the rule of law, and electoral fairness in a single stroke. We now know that a few minutes, a few feet, a few police officers, a handful of federal or state officials one way or the other could easily have produced a very different outcome.

Certainly if a strong, capable military leader had centrally coordinated the efforts of white supremacists, Proud Boys, 3 Percenters, and others; if they had arrested or assassinated members of Congress; or seized the Electoral College ballots; or exploded the pipe bombs they had planted, or created any number of violent pretexts for declaring martial law and blamed them on antifa — any of these acts could have been enough to shift the U.S. from electoral democracy to electoral dictatorship, from egalitarian diversity to white domination, from majority to minority rule, from reliance on law and facts to reliance on force and fraud. The realization that they could *actually* have destroyed democracy raises important questions, including:

1. What is it *exactly* that makes democracy so fragile? Is it possible for mediation and conflict resolution to make it less so? And if so, how might we de-escalate, settle, resolve, and prevent conflicts between highly polarized political opponents in ways that reduce the level of violence and hostility, both in rhetoric and in reality?
2. What would have happened if they had succeeded? What would we have done in response? Would *we* have become insurrectionists and attempted to defend democracy? How would our justifications for doing so have differed from theirs?
3. What are insurrections, putschs, and *coups d'état,* and where do they come from? How can we tell the difference between insurrections that *look* similar, and even have the same form, but differ entirely in their content? How is an insurrection to

overthrow democracy different from one that is organized to defend it?

4. What roles do political conflicts play in people's choices between different forms of government? In the fragility or robustness of democracies? In the willingness to accept fascistic, demagogic, corrupt, and authoritarian political systems?

5. What is the impact of political conflicts on bias, prejudice, and discrimination? On lying and propaganda? On hostility toward facts, reason, and science? On social inequality, economic inequity, and political autocracy? On the willingness to use mediation and conflict resolution in political disputes?

6. Is it possible for mediation, dialogue, consensus building, and other conflict resolution processes — not only to reinforce the rule of law, but to help us *evolve* beyond it? What would a *mediative* form of politics look like? What might mediators do to discourage political demonization, stereotyping, bias, and domination? To end the age-old battle of "Us" vs. "Them." To discourage the use of bullying, cruelty, and violence in political practices?

7. What might mediators do in response to fascistic behaviors on a personal, as well as a political level? In small-scale political arguments? Locally, as well as globally? How can we respond to intolerance and hatred without slipping into similar adversarial, undemocratic behaviors ourselves?

8. Is it possible for mediators to propose ways of discussing divisive political issues and conflicts that can shift us in the direction of dialogue, collaboration, consensus building, and joint problem solving? What are some of those ways?

9. What might mediators propose as ways of ensuring the accuracy and fairness of electoral outcomes? Of discouraging resort to violent and insurrectionary means? Of strengthening democracy and expanding it?

10. What can mediators and conflict resolvers do now and in the near future to prevent these conflicts from reappearing in

future elections, perhaps in more virulent and successful forms?

Before even beginning to consider these questions, it is necessary to concede that crimes have been committed, violence has been threatened and perpetrated, and lives have been lost on both sides. Constitutional processes have been abrogated, offices have been invaded, important papers have been stolen, and efforts have been made to overturn a fair and lawful election. These require a *legal* response, as without one, and in the absence of a collaborative replacement, we implicitly give permission for them to happen again.

Legal procedures were largely invented to discourage demagogues and tyrants by substituting *rights*-based formally "neutral" laws and adjudications for *power*-based entirely subjective dictations and fiats. Yet legal forms of conflict resolution nearly always fall short because they are objective, superficial, ceremonial, and oriented to compliance, and as a result, are not often successful in reaching people emotionally, attitudinally, or deeply, and rarely change their hearts or minds. Only *interest*-based methods do not *require* win/lose outcomes, and invite opposing parties to open their hearts and minds to each other and search together for better, deeper, more creative and mutually acceptable solutions.

These processes differ, of course, but there is no obvious reason why we cannot, as is common in litigated cases, adjudicate and mediate at the same time. To do so, we need to better understand the differences between power, rights, and interests, and think more deeply about insurrection and political conflict from a dispute resolution point of view. We need to reveal the connections between political conflicts and the rise of demagoguery and dictatorship, and design ways of preventing and resolving destructive political disputes by strengthening everyone's skills and capacities in democracy, collaboration, and mediation.

The difficulties, of course, lie in how we create the option of choosing one path over another, and in the details of how we go about discussing and resolving our differences. They lie in the complexity of separating free speech and legitimate political advocacy from the incitement to violent and aggressive actions that are aimed at abolishing democratic rights, or denying them to others altogether. Here, it is worth remembering, as Chief Justice Oliver Wendell Holmes explained, that it is not "shouting 'Fire'" that is beyond the protection of the First amendment, but *"falsely"* shouting "Fire" in a crowded theatre, and thereby causing a panic.

But what do we do when the fire *seems* to many to be real, or is believed to be real by a large number of voters — often because they were told it was real by demagogic leaders who *knew* it wasn't, yet promoted the false idea that it was for their own personal political ends? What would the appropriate *democratic* response be to an authoritarian, dictatorial takeover of government; to systematic suspension of the Constitutional right to vote; to the *actual* theft of an election?

One answer is insurrection. If the election *had* been successfully stolen by Q-Anon, Proud Boys, 3 Percenters, and others, would not Biden voters have believed themselves justified in using "extra-electoral" mass-insurgency tactics against the forcible installation of a second Trump presidency, as nearly all of us believe such actions would have been justified against Hitler?

In other words, the problem is *not* that there was a mass demonstration seeking to compel government officials to recognize the electoral will of the people, but that extra-electoral, insurrectionary means were used to hijack a *legitimate* election, prevent the will of a majority of the people from being recognized, and undermine popular democracy by repudiating and potentially dismantling it.

During World War II, Albert Camus advocated insurrection as a legitimate form of opposition to the rule of fascists and a direct expression of democracy, writing:

What is an insurrection? It is the people in arms. Who are the people?
They are those in a nation who will never be made to kneel.

Demagogues, dictators, and tyrants throughout history have
routinely risen and held on to power through the use of violence and
hatred, turning one group against another in order to divide and
conquer, dominate and control, exploit and oppress; and by
overturning elections and triggering insurrections in response. As
Joseph Stalin cynically observed,

> It is enough that the people know there was an election. The people
> who cast the votes decide nothing. The people who count the votes
> decide everything.

"Insurrection" is, of course, a label that has not only legal, but moral,
political, and emotional meanings. The danger of labeling one's
opponents in any conflict, especially political conflict, is that doing
so generates stereotypes that encourage assumptions of evil,
undermine democracy, obstruct dialogue, turn animosity in a circle,
replicate enmity and hatred, and reproduce chronic, engrained,
unending conflicts, and moral justifications for exclusion and
violence.

Yet it is critical to the life and vitality of any democracy that it *not*
prevent the expression of dissent and diverse political views, even
extreme ones, or regard polarizations and passions as problematic,
but instead ask questions that draw adversaries into dialogue,
collaborative negotiation, social problem solving, and mediation, all
of which invite them to participate in democratic processes and
relationships that recognize and seek to satisfy everyone's legitimate
interests, acknowledge and respond constructively to each other's
emotions, and work together for the common good.

To achieve these ends, we need to think carefully about how to
define the problem. For instance, while many journalists and
politicians continue to characterize the problem as one of
"populism," this term conceals an anti-democratic bias by implying

that popular participation in politics and electoral passions are inherently dangerous and ought to be discouraged or prevented. Blame is thereby placed on citizens, rather than on demagogic politicians who routinely lie to, manipulate, and take advantage of them in order to win office.

Labeling those who act outside the political consensus as "populist" reflects a fear of social movements and genuine political change, and encourages a distrust of democracy. An alternative approach would focus on the use of dishonest and manipulative propaganda by demagogues and would-be tyrants, discourage corruption and dishonesty within the political system, and design dispute resolution systems that actively seek to reduce and prevent hatred and violence, while at the same time promoting direct citizen participation in political activity.

Populism naturally assumes different forms and will express itself more violently in power-based political systems; more litigiously in rights-based systems; and more collaboratively in interest-based systems, where constructive channels can be designed and widely used to encourage popular participation in facilitated problem definition, analysis, debate, dialogue, brainstorming, consensus building, negotiation, mediation, voting, action planning, and implementation.

As mediators, it is important for us to consider how we might bring a range of methods to bear on political conflicts, in an effort – not to deny, water down, or compromise genuine differences, or even to simply acknowledge that they exist, but at a deeper level, to reveal their origins in "things" rather than "people" – i.e., in disruptive technological and environmental changes; intensifying global challenges to increasingly outdated and dysfunctional social, economic, and political systems; and a growing need for innovative, collaborative, interest-based methods for preventing, resolving, moving through, transforming, transcending, and evolving beyond the chronic sources of political conflicts.

In these ways, mediative methodologies encourage democracy *itself* to advance, improve, and evolve beyond adversarial power- and rights-based forms by introducing collaborative, interest-based, "omni-partial" techniques, such as informal problem solving, consensus building, teamwork, collaborative negotiation, dialogue, non-violent communication, restorative justice, circles, and mediation, all of which combine objective and subjective, substantive and procedural, mind and heart, as approaches to achieving outcomes that are not *unavoidably* win/lose, thereby strengthening empathy, direct participation, solidarity, and authentic agreement.

Indeed, it is possible to use mediative methodologies, such as "conflict resolution systems design," to identify the systemic elements that generate chronic political conflicts and imagine interest-based alternatives that invite dialogue and strengthen large group multi-party consensus building processes. For example, it is possible for mediators, dialogue facilitators, conflict coaches, and others to convene and work with groups of political adversaries to:

1. Jointly agree on a small set of basic principles that would govern future elections, such as "every adult citizen shall have a right to vote," or "every vote shall be counted."
2. Invite a team of mathematicians, engineers, political scientists, leaders of high-tech companies, and others to reach consensus recommendations on secure and accurate tools that allow people to vote by mail-in ballot or computer while eliminating the possibility of *anyone* stealing an election.
3. Initiate facilitated dialogues in diverse neighborhoods and communities to elicit consensus-based recommendations on improved ways of conducting elections more collaboratively, fairly, non-violently, and securely.
4. Establish federal, state, city and county Ombuds offices to investigate and resolve electoral conflicts, with teams of mediators and facilitators available to meet with candidates, representatives of political parties, and others before, during, and after elections to prevent and resolve any conflicts that

may arise, and encourage mediation and rapid resolution of electoral disputes.

5. Create a branch of the Justice Department that is isolated from political influence dedicated to protecting and enforcing voting rights, with the power to record contested votes for subsequent determination.

In addition, conflict resolution professionals can design, organize, and facilitate multi-track dialogues, joint factual investigations, "exploratory exchanges," and "courageous conversations" between political adversaries regarding issues, for example, such as whether the 2020 election was in fact stolen, or how to address highly contested time-dependent issues, like responses to Covid-19. These dialogues can easily be designed in ways that encourage mass participation in practical political decision-making, and not just voting for candidates, but reaching consensus on policies, legislation, and proposals for action.

It is even possible to design dialogues that draw proponents of the most fantastic conspiracy theories and paranoid imaginings into open conversation and encourage joint participation in factual scrutiny and a mutual search for falsifiability, through a sometimes meticulous, painstaking process of asking questions, discussing, investigating, experimenting, and exploring alternatives.

In spite of the potential impact of these ideas and proposals, it is likely that global social, economic, political, and environmental conflicts will continue to escalate, polarizing political factions, and demanding that we choose between dramatically different futures and outcomes. The most urgent and pressing of these conflicts concern access to vaccines and health care, global warming and environmental destruction, migration and poverty, nuclear proliferation and brinksmanship, war and famine, and many others.

Alongside and beneath these pressing conflicts lie deeper issues, including the continued domination of countries in the South by those in the North; dismantling the systemic sources of bias and intolerance; mitigating the destructive impact of vast disparities of wealth; overcoming limited access to medical care, food, and water; agreeing on the proper role of police and military forces; assessing the continued viability of globally unregulated capitalism; the social impact of innovative technologies, and many others that urgently require our long-term global cooperation.

Clearly, the underlying political conflicts that make it difficult for us to solve these problems are not going to disappear, and intensely adversarial political conflicts are *guaranteed* to re-emerge rapidly, and on a national scale, at least by the 2024 presidential election — especially if Kamala Harris chooses to run for President, and Donald Trump decides to do the same. The electorate and the Senate are now nearly evenly divided between Democrats and Republicans, with millions of voters suspicious and distrustful of each other, and few signs of any willingness to work, or even talk, to one another.

Yet, for this very reason, the need for people who are skilled in a broad range of dispute resolution techniques and processes has never been greater. Most importantly, the skills that are required to strengthen collaborative, democratic, and mediative political problem solving are *exactly* those that conflict resolution professionals practice successfully, on a smaller scale, every day.

Every political conflict encourages us to pick sides and choose between alternate universes, which increasingly narrow down to options of either/or, yes or no, this or that, him or her, left or right, party A or party B, forward or backward. Yet in making these choices, we collapse complex, nuanced, multi-dimensional, analog problems into simplistic, flattened, lower dimensional, digital choices that *seem* to require adversarial, win/lose outcomes. Worse, they force us to choose between selfishness and sharing, competition and collaboration, looking out for ourselves and caring for others, when it is actually possible for us to do both.

Political conflicts ask us to add our weight and energy, our hearts and minds, bodies, and brains to bring about the future we want; but they do so by seemingly requiring us to fight for *our* future over and against the futures of others, so that our victory automatically spells their defeat. Yet it is possible for us to decide instead to unite with each other and face our common problems; to engage in dialogue with those who desire different futures and synthesize our best ideas; to discover the deeper reasons for polarization in the multi-faceted complexity and subtlety of our problems; to recognize that all conflicts conceal underlying truths; and to agree that we will do our very best to make sure we leave no one behind.

If we are to turn democracy and political conflict in a more collaborative, interest-based, problem-solving direction, we will require higher order skills, processes, forms of communication, and relational capacities. These, in turn, will require a greater appreciation for diversity, dissent, and doubt; a higher tolerance for ambiguity, complexity, subtlety, and transparency; and an expanded competence in collaboration, dialogue, consensus building, and mediation, which will allow us to invite citizens of all cultures, beliefs, and backgrounds to join one another in solving common problems *without* over-simplifying or blaming them on each other. All of this is possible, and it is *already being done*, every day, in the small-scale work of conflict resolution practitioners.

Because of what took place on January 6, and the passion and intensity of the political conflicts that led to it, we can now understand what is at stake, and we do not have long to prepare for 2022 and 2024. We have listened, watched, read, argued, and voted, and thereby brought the official, customary, traditional electoral process to a close. Yet it is only now that *real* politics can begin, and that genuine democracy can become possible — perhaps in ways that will allow us, as mediators, to elicit and help shape the conversations and interactions that lay the foundations for the kind of world that we, our children, and our grandchildren's grandchildren will want to live in.

Whatever we do, whichever path we take, our actions and inactions shape the unseen channels through which our political futures, and those of succeeding generations, will flow. Through our willingness to apply our skills, and aid even our opponents in collaborating and solving their problems, we can help design and create the processes and relationships, cultures and contexts, systems, and environments, that will be needed for all of us to survive, and not sink into brutal, violent, senseless, and barbaric conflicts.

Each of us can offer hope or withhold it. We can face our problems together, or grapple with them alone. We can open our hearts or shut them to one another. Every day, whether we intend to or not, we create a path forward. We impact and participate in political conflicts. We act as citizens. We *vote*. So, let's vote for a less hostile, violent, and adversarial world. Let's vote for dialogue, problem solving, and conflict resolution. The time is short, and every day, every act, every vote counts. Especially yours.

14

20 PROPOSALS TO RESOLVE ELECTORAL CONFLICTS AND STRENGTHEN DEMOCRACY

E lectoral democracy has gone through a period of profound conflicts, yet each unique conflict points us toward potential solutions and more collaborative processes. Here are 20 proposals to help resolve electoral conflicts between political parties, fortify voting rights, improve trust in outcomes, strengthen democracy, encourage dialogue between differing groups and factions, and promote participation in political decision-making, based on the core democratic principles of popular sovereignty, majority rule, and minority rights.

1. In advance of elections, initiate facilitated dialogues in diverse local neighborhoods and communities to increase communication and understanding, and elicit consensus-based recommendations for ways of conducting upcoming elections more collaboratively, fairly, and securely.
2. Create a bi-partisan national electoral commission to summarize popular input, synthesize ideas, reach consensus, and recommend improved rules and processes, including minimal standards for electoral fairness for all elections, including those in states, cities, and counties.

3. Invite representatives of opposing political parties and factions to meet, aided by professional mediators and facilitators, to discuss, collaboratively negotiate, and reach consensus on the rules that will govern elections, including the conduct of candidates during debates, ethical campaign ads, limits on financial contributions, ways of reducing fraud and dishonesty, resolving contested outcomes, and accepting final results.

4. Establish and enforce a Voter's Bill of Rights that guarantees one person/one vote as a universal right of all citizens, including those with felony convictions.

5. Establish automatic, life-long voter registration for all citizens, based on a commonly used form of identification, such as social security or drivers' license numbers.

6. Permit and protect mail-in ballots and advance voting, and require that all such votes be counted in advance of in-person voting, wherever possible.

7. Require that voting machines be secure, non-hackable, manufactured by non-partisan companies or agencies, and capable of creating a paper trail.

8. Fund the development of free, secure, easy-to-use apps that inform citizens of their voting rights, provide multiple forums for facilitated dialogues and discussion of the issues, enable fact-checking, support on-line dispute resolution where requested, and permit on-line voting, making sure there is access to computers and internet for those without.

9. Re-conduct the census to ensure that everyone is counted, including immigrant and homeless citizens, so that future elections and seats in Congress can be distributed accurately and fairly.

10. Initiate in-person and on-line dialogues and town-hall meetings in local communities following candidate debates, led by professional mediators and facilitators, in which participants are asked to discuss and reach consensus on recommended solutions to issues raised during the debates,

as well as ways of improving both debate and dialogue processes.

11. Tighten restrictions on private, special interest, and foreign campaign contributions, and on all electorally related contributions to candidates or PACs above a mutually agreed-upon amount.

12. Shorten the electoral timetable, and provide public funding for federal campaign ads, with a precondition, that these be fact-checked, and candidate approved prior to airing.

13. End the Electoral College, or its ability of to disregard the popular vote, or revise its rules to ensure fairness and respect the principle of "one-person/one vote," and legislatively block partisan state legislatures from altering electoral outcomes or overturning the popular vote.

14. Use mathematical modeling, artificial intelligence, and community and public policy mediation to identify, restrict, and repair gerrymandering, and make it easier for citizens to challenge electoral boundaries in court.

15. Improve, automate, and streamline the process for recounting ballots, using neutral or bipartisan observers wherever outcomes are contested, and mitigate winner-take-all elections by using percentage or proportional representation, instant runoff voting (allowing second choice votes to count) fusion voting (allowing two or more parties to nominate the same candidate), and similar methods.

16. Pass legislation making election days partial national holidays, with paid time off to enable those who work to vote.

17. Prohibit taxation without representation, by allowing everyone who is taxed to vote and be represented in Congress, including residents of the District of Columbia and Puerto Rico, should they so desire.

18. Create a branch of the Justice Department that is isolated from political influence to protect and enforce voting rights, with the power to record contested votes for subsequent determination and counting.

19. Establish federal, state, city, and county Ombuds offices to investigate and resolve electoral conflicts, with teams of mediators and facilitators who convene candidates and representatives of political parties in an effort to prevent and resolve conflicts that arise before, during, and after elections; and encourage them to mediate these issues before going to court.

20. After elections are over, invite people in diverse neighborhoods and communities to participate in on-line and in-person dialogues to evaluate the electoral process, reach consensus on recommendations for future elections, and discuss ways of healing, reuniting, and commit to working together to solve common problems, using restorative justice circles, and facilitated "truth and reconciliation" types of processes.

15

IMPROVING COMMUNICATIONS ON-LINE

AN ITERATIVE CONFLICT COACHING EXPERIENCE BY ZOOM AND EMAIL

Here are several nearly verbatim emails I exchanged following mediations between "Rachel" (whose divorce from "Mark" I mediated years earlier) and "John," with whom she had been having an affair, until it stopped when he returned to his prior girlfriend, "Sally." Due to the pandemic, the entire coaching process took place by Zoom and email. It was published in Michael Lang and Peter Nicholson's book, Family Conflict During a Pandemic: Stories of Struggle and Hope.

Hi Ken,

Since the last time we saw each other ... I've ebbed and flowed through the ordeal with John ...

I had this epiphany today that maybe the last part of the healing will come if I look at this differently. I've survived the worst when it comes to the heartache. BUT it's hard to move on to the thriving part.

[On Zoom, I asked her to draft an email to send to John.]

First draft:

> I get it.
>
> The message is clear.
>
> I promise to go away.
>
> I'm sorry that I haven't honored your need for total distance.
>
> Some day... when you look back on this... if you have the capacity for empathy... you will understand. You went back to someone you love. Maybe if you think about when you lost Sally... It's hard to be alone and face the world from the place of feeling discarded. I know you think Mark left me on the curb... well you put me in the trash. I'm lucky I got my body back and I'm grateful for this year by myself because I'm learning about me and trust me... I know it's not pretty. I hope you are truly happy because you've finally lost me.

[On Zoom, I asked her to go over her draft, imagine how John would read it, and revise it.]

Second draft:

> I'm sorry that I haven't honored your need for total distance.
>
> Some day... when you look back on this... you will understand. It's hard to be alone and face the world from the place of feeling discarded. I'm grateful for this year by myself.
>
> I'm learning about me.
>
> I hope you are truly happy.

[I emailed back: "Thanks for sending me your redraft. Now start over and ask yourself two questions: 1. If I were John, what would I most want to hear Rachel say to me? Write that. And 2. If I were completely free from his narcissism, my addiction, and the "heroin rush" of contacting him you described on our call, what would I want/need to say to him? Write that, then reread the earlier drafts and see what comes up."]

[Rachel wrote back:]

> Thank you so much! I will work on a new draft. It's interesting that I completely understand this draft will be harder to write. It allows for me to be more mindful. Taking away manipulation and compulsivity. This is probably the hardest task you've given me.

Third Draft:

> John
>
> I want you to know that I cherish the time we spent together. You are an incredible trainer and our time working out and eating eggs and pancakes after our weekly sessions is a good memory. You were infectious in that gym and taught me to enjoy working out.
>
> More importantly, I am grateful to you for stepping in and helping me and the girls during a very difficult time in our lives. I will always remember you for your kindness and how you pushed me to be a better me… when it came to my fears and habits.
>
> I wish I could have loved you the way you wanted me to. I am happy you have found love and I want all good things for you.
>
> I want to respect your need for privacy and will not reach out to you and your family anymore.

I wrote back:

> Beautiful Rachel, well done. Now read your earlier drafts and write down what you learned by doing this, how you felt, who you became with each draft, and how your conflict shifted as a result.

16

20 WAYS TO IMPROVE UNITED NATIONS MEETINGS AND CLIMATE CHANGE NEGOTIATIONS

In preparation for the next international meeting on climate change in Glasgow in November 2021, it is important to begin thinking together, not only about outcomes, but ways of improving the process of meeting, discussing, and negotiating agreements on climate change.

Mediators, facilitators, ombudsmen, and other conflict resolution professionals have had considerable experience designing effective problem solving, communication, negotiation, and conflict resolution processes over several decades, and based on my experience as a mediator and observer at the Copenhagen Conference of the Parties, it is possible for the United Nations Framework Convention on Climate Change (UNFCCC), without significant financial investment, to improve the quality of its meetings and negotiations in Glasgow and beyond, in at least the following 20 ways:

1. Conduct in-depth, broadly inclusive, collaborative evaluations of the process used in Copenhagen, Paris, and other climate change meetings to identify what worked and what can be improved
2. Consult widely with diverse public and private sector

organizations and individuals who have experience designing negotiation/dispute resolution systems and can provide ways of improving the entire negotiation process

3. Develop a comprehensive set of process recommendations for future talks, secure agreement to implement them prior to the session, and brief delegates on them before they arrive

4. Create international negotiation and conflict resolution protocols, model mediation language, and annexes to existing agreements that encourage a broad range of collaborative interest-based dispute resolution processes, including mediation, ombudsmen, facilitated dialogue, and other methods

5. Ask each delegation to future talks to include among their members one or more trained mediators, collaborative negotiators, ombudsmen, or small group facilitators who can assist in bridging differences as they occur

6. Assign one or more UN mediators or ombudsmen to every delegation, and to each small group and problem-solving meeting

7. Appoint facilitators, ombudsmen, and mediators in advance for every meeting and asking them to recommend ways of improving the next one

8. Send experienced negotiators, facilitators, ombudsmen, and mediators to meet with the parties in advance of conferences and negotiating sessions to help set targets and timetables, and encourage compromises that could lead to better and quicker agreements

9. Drastically simplify and reduce the rigidity and formality of protocols, rules, and official processes, especially as they effect the negotiation and agreement writing process

10. Shorten large meetings and break participants up into small, diverse, informal teams to brainstorm alternatives, agree on common goals or shared values, and reach consensus recommendations on specific problems, led by facilitators and mediators

11. Offer free trainings throughout the process for individuals,

delegations and teams in collaborative negotiation, facilitation, and conflict resolution

12. Reach agreement on a variety of next steps that can be taken when consensus is not reached, including dialogue, informal problem solving, collaborative negotiation, and mediation

13. Appoint fast-forming, diverse problem-solving teams with experts from all nations, regions, groups, types of alternatives and ranges of opinion, with professional facilitators and recorders to aid them in their work

14. Periodically conduct process checks to make sure everything is on track and make improvements as needed

15. Facilitate meetings of climate change experts and scientists to develop consensus-based recommendations, include them on problem solving teams, and convene meetings of diverse specialists to advise delegates on specific topics

16. Conduct frequent open dialogue sessions on critical topics without at first attempting to reach agreement, provide multiple opportunities for free-ranging small group discussions, and repeatedly elicit recommendations for better ways of reaching consensus

17. Focus not only on reaching a single comprehensive agreement, but also on reaching smaller, specialized, limited, tentative, provisional, national, regional and bloc agreements, then work to accumulate and amalgamate them into a single comprehensive draft

18. Allow facilitators to stop the process if it isn't working, discuss what isn't working openly, invite suggestions, and propose ways of improving it

19. Consider the entire multi-year agreement drafting process as a conflict *system,* and use conflict resolution systems design principles to develop better ways of responding to obstacles, impasses and conflicts as they occur

20. Continue to search for ongoing, diverse preventative measures that can be adopted by all parties and UN organizations, that will help reduce the severity of future problems

17

RACE AND CASTE, GENDER AND PATRIARCHY, WEALTH AND CLASS:

MEDIATING THE SYSTEMS, STRUCTURES, AND SOURCES OF PREJUDICE

The function, the very serious function of racism, . . . is distraction. It keeps you from doing your work. It keeps you explaining, over and over again, your reason for being. Somebody says you have no language and you spend twenty years proving that you do. Somebody says your head isn't shaped properly so you have scientists working on the fact that it is. Somebody says you have no art, so you dredge that up. Somebody says you have no kingdoms, so you dredge that up. None of this is necessary. There will always be one more thing.

— TONI MORRISON

Only very slowly and late have men come to realize that unless freedom is universal it is only extended privilege.

— CHRISTOPHER HILL

It is not permissible that the authors of devastation should also be innocent. It is the innocence which constitutes the crime.

— JAMES BALDWIN

A s a society, we have spent enormous amounts of time engaged in bitter conflicts, hostile debates, and adversarial exchanges over racism and policing, sexism and sexual harassment, homophobia and gay marriage, anti-Semitism and Islamophobia, immigration and border walls, poverty and homelessness, trans athletes and gendered bathrooms, America First and global warming, Civil War statues and teaching about slavery, accusations and denials of bias, stereotyping, prejudice, and discrimination, and similar issues.

Each of these has fueled intense arguments and adversarial exchanges between increasingly intolerant and polarized opponents, including Democrats and Republicans, Black Lives Matter and Proud Boys, mask wearers and Covid deniers; proponents and detractors of mail-in ballots, online voting, and voter ID cards; advocates of renewable energy and fans of fossil fuels; champions of globalization and promoters of tariffs, supporters and critics of gun control, gay marriage, defunding police, morning after pills, sanctuary cities, reparations, and similar issues.

We have not resolved *any* of these disputes, or convinced each other, or even discussed them intelligently, but ended up instead screaming at one another, clashing violently, and being prepared to manipulate, and even jettison the entire democratic process if it doesn't back the candidates and policies we support. As a result, we have become deeply divided, hostile, suspicious, and less able to work together to solve pressing common problems. Yet we are *inextricably* bound together, not only in neighborhoods and communities, language, and citizenship, but by our common humanity, and a growing range of worries that threaten our survival and require our cooperation.

Some of the increasing intensity of these conflicts comes from the fact that far-reaching, fundamental changes are taking place in the world, rekindling ancient prejudices, resurrecting outdated paradigms, transforming once settled relationships, blinding us to what is obvious, and shifting the very ground on which we live. Many of the technologies and forms of communication, along with the attitudes and assumptions, skills and methodologies, systems and structures, processes and relationships from earlier times have simply disappeared, or no longer work, or are seen as biased, unjust, ineffective, and damaging, leaving many people feeling disregarded and left behind.

At the same time, advances in science, economic inter-dependency, world travel and connectedness, access to diverse local and global cultures, and increasing openness to cross-cultural relationships have intensified the need for higher order communication, negotiation, and conflict resolution skills. Yet these have often lagged, or been trivialized, or regarded as "touchy-feely," and actively resisted by those who have found themselves unable or unwilling to keep up.

More problematically, the media, methods, and modalities for communicating and resolving cross-racial, cross-gender, cross-class, and cross-cultural conflicts; the skills, capacities, and attitudes for respectfully and collaboratively negotiating with each other; and the *willingness* — even to constructively listen, talk about, and solve life-threatening difficulties, or grapple with the ambiguity and complexity of diversity, dissent, collaboration, and change, have not kept pace with the scale, scope, and complexity of our problems, or been applied adequately and comprehensively, or been used to design the systems and structures that might prevent them at their source.

As a result, our political conversations have become spiteful, distracted, stifled, and unable to address the real issues. We have not discovered even the *language* we need to connect these conflicts, reveal their underlying symmetries, or point the way to fresh ideas and syntheses. This, I think, is where we need to begin, and there is no better, or more important place to do so than with conflicts regarding race, which lie at the center of the passion and emotion experienced by people on both sides of the political divide.

A First Step: Race and Caste Distinguished

The language currently being used to discuss race, gender, wealth, religion, and similar social divisions, not only in the U.S., but everywhere, consists largely of stereotypes, slurs, accusations, threats, calls to violence, shaming, castigation, and condemnation. These *automatically* generate denial, defensiveness, and counter-attack, along with evasiveness, euphemism, deceit, condescension, disrespect, and rationalization, which routinely re-trigger the first set of responses, causing the argument to turn in a circle and go nowhere, except downhill.

A first step in the direction of improved communication, dialogue, problem solving, collaborative negotiation, and conflict resolution is to *redefine* the problem in ways that make the experience of bias and pre-judgment more universal; that encourage empathy and honesty to flow more freely; that deepen our understanding of what lies *beneath* these conflicts; that clarify what connects all forms of prejudice; that explain the passion and intense emotion that surround it; and that help us figure out how to talk to one another and work together to solve the problem of how to solve our problems.

In 2020, the Pulitzer Prize winning author Isabel Wilkerson published a brilliant, beautifully crafted, groundbreaking book, *Caste: The Origins of Our Discontents*, in which she distinguished race and racism from caste and casteism. Offering examples from many different countries and historical periods, she defined caste in an interesting and useful way:

> Caste is the granting or withholding of respect, status, honor, attention, privileges, resources, benefit of the doubt, and human kindness to someone on the basis of their perceived rank or standing in the hierarchy … Caste is insidious and therefore powerful because it is not hatred, it is not personal. It is the worn grooves of comforting routines and unthinking expectations, patterns of a social order that has been in place for so long that it looks like the natural order of things.

The difference between castes-ism and racism, she pointed out, is not always easy to identify, as these categories are "interwoven," yet can be described as follows:

> Any action or institution that mocks, harms, assumes, or attaches inferiority or stereotype on the basis of the social construct of race can be considered racism. Any action or structure that seeks to limit, hold back, or put someone in a defined ranking, seeks to keep someone in their place by elevating or denigrating that person on the basis of their perceived category, can be seen as casteism.

Wilkerson went further, and made the essential distinction between them clear:

> [C]aste does not allow us to ignore structure. Caste *is* structure. Caste is ranking. Caste is the boundaries that reinforce the fixed assignments based on what people look like…. To achieve a truly egalitarian world requires looking deeper than what we think we see. We cannot win against a hologram …

Or, more simply still, "Caste is the bones, race the skin." And, in a passage that helps us understand what lies deeper, and points to the chronic source, explanatory principle, and point of origin of both casteism and racism, she wrote:

> Casteism is the investment in keeping the hierarchy as it is … [or reinforcing it] to maintain your own ranking, advantage, privilege, [in order] to elevate yourself above others or keep others beneath you.

The great value of Wilkerson's work is that it offers a deep explanation of the connections between race and other forms of bias, and of their relationship to conflict resolution, and to the larger conflicts we are experiencing regarding social inequality, economic inequity, political autocracy, and ecological destruction. She offers a clear perspective through the lens of hierarchy, with its associated survival fears and desires for domination and superiority, into the *universal* experience of bias and prejudice.

Caste is maintained through what Wilkerson describes as a set of eight "pillars" or principles that can be found in Indian castes, Nazi Germany's Nuremberg laws, South African apartheid, and U.S. segregation, among others. These include, as I see them, a set of systemic supports and justifications that enforce inheritability, ban intermarriage, permit rape, protect genetic "purity," prohibit fair competition, legitimize stereotypes and slurs, authorize terror as a means of enforcement and cruelty as a means of control, and inculcate an ideology of innate superiority and inferiority.

In these ways, caste *invents* "untouchables," whose physical *being* is regarded as corrupt, filthy, disgusting, and disease-ridden. These lead to segregated, apartheid-style seating areas, separate drinking fountains and bathrooms, and the emptying of entire swimming pools that have been integrated. These pillars further separate people, increase their ignorance of one another, magnify their fear of physical contact, erect elaborate defenses against empathy and compassion, and give rise to a wide range of racist behaviors, leading to the theft of dignity and happiness, lives and labor, power and possessions, peace and justice – and finally, to murder, rape, and genocide.

These outcomes are grounded in the perception that hierarchical, fiercely competitive, "zero-sum," "win/lose," "power-based" methods *have* to be adopted due to scarce resources, limited entitlements, and restricted access to status, wealth, power, and ecological advantage. This leads to the pervasive assumption that "social-Darwinian," "survival of the fittest," "fight to the death" tactics are essential if we want to avoid *personal* loss, defeat, enslavement, and death, and that we need to defend ourselves, our families, and those we believe are like us, against those who would take what is ours.

But what is this perception, other than the outward appearance of our own fear and selfishness, anger and self-doubt, guilt and shame, panic and pain? What is it, other than our subconscious awareness that the entire *construct* of white, male, wealthy, straight, etc. superiority is a *sham*, together with a desire for release through catharsis and annihilation of the Other, whose very *presence* reminds us of the fraudulence of our claim? What is it, other than our own stunted capacity for empathy and compassion; our lack of skill in relating to those who are different; our difficulty tolerating ambiguity, diversity, and dissent; our anticipation of rejection by others; our suppressed belief that we are unworthy; our unspoken desire for acceptance, affirmation, and affection; for relationship, resolution, redemption, and reconciliation?

4 Levels of Bias, Stereotyping, Prejudice, and Discrimination

Extending Wilkerson's distinction between race and caste, we can imagine a number of equally important distinctions — for example, between gender and patriarchy; wealth and class; patriotism and jingoism, religious belief and ultra-orthodoxy, sexual orientation and homophobia, political principles and dogmatism, etc., each pointing to a set of deeper, broader, less personal and behavioral, and more systemic or structural supports; and to still deeper, more divisive and universal underlying causes.

The goal of these distinctions is not to diminish the very real impact of racism, sexism, classism, homophobia, and other forms of bias, stereotyping, prejudice, and discrimination, but rather to deepen them, to reveal them as *emergent*, and therefore, *relatively* superficial, interpersonal, communicative and behavioral *manifestations* of much more fundamental and longer lasting underpinnings and chronic sources. This allows us to see that *all* the conflicts that surround all the different forms of bias, stereotyping, prejudice, and discrimination exist *simultaneously* on three distinct levels:

1. The internal, *personal* level of *biases* and emotions, consisting largely of rapid neurophysiological reactions to perceived differences, hostile intentions, and potential threats; together with received ideas, personal memories, social memes, and physical responses to stress

2. The direct, immediate, *interpersonal* level of *communications* and relational behaviors, which can be expressed overtly or covertly through racial slurs, stereotypes, and "dog whistle" euphemisms; directly or indirectly through hatred, rejection, and disrespect; aggressively or passively through violence, ostracism, and distancing; and in countless other ways

3. The deeper *structural* and *systemic* level of *caste*, patriarchy, class, etc., as relational, organizational, and institutional efforts to reinforce domination and superiority of some over others; keep specific groups and categories of people in their place; and punish those who cross lines, or do not "know their place"

4. The still deeper *source* of these behaviors, systems, and structures at the *algorithmic*, or "encoded" level, that invisibly connects all forms of bias, stereotyping, prejudice, and discrimination through the perceived need to maintain or improve one's position in a social, economic, political, or ecological hierarchy by dominating others and avoiding being dominated by them

At the first, personal level, inside all of us are a number of largely unconscious biases, pre-judgments and emotionally charged responses to people and circumstances that are grounded in experience and influenced by social conditioning, yet for the most part go unexamined.

At the second, interpersonal level, bias, stereotyping, prejudice, and discrimination are expressed in a broad range of communications and behaviors, statements and actions that range from simplistic stereotypes, subtle slurs, and "micro-aggressions" to apartheid and lynching; from silly jokes and clumsy come-ons to sexual harassment and rape; from casual closeting remarks to gender shaming and imprisonment; from petty anti-Semitic slights to genocide. The rationalizations offered by those who say these things and engage in these actions reveal that they are sometimes simply *tests* to see how far they can go before they are stopped, or backwards justifications for hostile, anti-social behaviors that would otherwise be seen as shameful, cruel, and inhuman.

At the third, deeper level lie the systems and structures that support bias, stereotyping, prejudice, and discrimination; that evoke and trigger, but do not *require*, insulting comments or antagonistic behaviors directed at others. Instead, they offer the *appearance* (to those engaging in them) of being logical, neutral, and unbiased. These prejudicial systems and structures rely on distinctions based on "facts," yet fail to recognize that these facts are themselves the result of *centuries* of disparate treatment, and invented, often unconsciously, in an effort to *create* facts that match the stereotype, and thereby "reverse engineer" the evidence, moral rationalizations, and justifications needed for domination to succeed. Thus, people are denied work, then described as lazy; impoverished, then called dirty; shamed, then scorned as shameless.

Thus, reducing funding for largely minority public schools predictably results in their students being less likely to learn, be admitted to college, or receive higher paying jobs. Indeed, the simple reluctance of any system to take account of a history and legacy of *past* bias, stereotyping, prejudice, and discrimination — together with an unwillingness to make reparations or change directions — will *automatically* result in continued unfairness, domination, and prejudice. All any system needs to turn in a circle is selective amnesia, a pretense of neutrality, and acceptance of an unequal *status quo*.

This predictability and automaticity lead us to the fourth, still deeper, *algorithmic*, causal or encoded level, and the *source* of these systems and structures, communications and behaviors. An algorithm is simply a rule, a set of instructions, an operating system, or a mathematical function that gives rise to repetitive outcomes. Fear, for example, is a simple, *repeatable* neurophysiological algorithm that begins with a perceived threat, followed by a rapid response in the amygdala, triggering a cascade of chemical reactions we now call the "fight, flight, freeze, or fawn" reaction.

At this deeper, algorithmic level, bias, stereotyping, prejudice, and discrimination take the form of a simple, elementary rule that governs *every* hierarchy: those who are above are permitted to dominate and control, exploit and oppress, eat first and prevail over, injure and even exterminate, those who are below. As a consequence, all are arrayed along a vertical one-dimensional line in order of their social status, economic wealth, political power, or ecological advantage; or their age, height, or weight; speed or strength; mathematical ability or emotional intelligence; color or gender; religion or politics; or any other criteria we may select based on our needs and values, likes and dislikes, desires and fears, histories and antagonisms. Ambiguity and confusion are then banished, along with insecurity and fear of loss — at least in the short run and for those who are above — but always at a price.

The central purpose of this underlying algorithm or code is to establish and maintain competitive, adversarial, hierarchical, zero sum principles as the core "operating system," fundamental axioms, design criteria, ground rules, and blueprints needed to guide the creation and continued iteration of a complex set of multi-layered, self-reinforcing systems and structures, processes and relationships, attitudes and assumptions, communications and behaviors, actions and reactions, that separate and rank people from top to bottom, then grant privileges and measure lives accordingly.

Systems and structures are needed to implement the algorithm; to identify those who do not "belong" and separate them from those who do; to marginalize and punish those who dissent or seek to change the system; to appear to "fairly" apportion and distribute rewards to winners and punishments to losers; to create *superficially* neutral, "color blind," non-prejudicial rationalizations for targeting people based on their identities or differences, which can be communicated by simple catch phrases and euphemisms.

Biased interpersonal communications and behaviors are then needed to coerce compliance with these systems and structures; to monitor and enforce segregations and exclusions; to promote personal bullying, shaming, ostracism, humiliation, and violence; to encourage fear, undermine empathy, and implant self-doubt and self-hatred; to rationalize, divert, disguise, moderate, and deny the truth; and to paper over any underlying guilt, residual empathy, or lingering shame caused by doing so.

The Algorithm: Prejudice, Domination, and the Zero-Sum Game

In 1944, mathematician John von Neumann and economist Oskar Morgenstern published their classic *Theory of Games and Economic Behavior,* in which they created a foundation for understanding the strategic implications of competitive, or "zero-sum;" and cooperative, or "non-zero sum" interactions called "games" that took place between several people, or "players," who may be either individuals or groups.

A zero-sum game is one in which, out of a total of 10, if I get 7, you get 3; and if I get 8, you get 2. Zero sum games are commonly referred to as "conflict games," because negotiations are inevitably competitive, adversarial, and distributive, there is a "fixed pie" that cannot be expanded, and these, in combination, generate chronic conflicts. War and genocide can then be seen as "natural" "final solutions" to any zero-sum social, economic, political, or ecological game, because the dominant person or group simply seeks to "zero out" the sum by taking everything and eliminate competitors.

Bias, stereotyping, prejudice, and discrimination can therefore be seen as *essential* elements in every zero-sum game, as they undermine collaborative inclinations and assumptions, justify maximizing my/our share, and strengthen my/our competitive advantage. Yet they always, ultimately, and inexorably seek to zero out others, and therefore gravitate toward aggression, violence, and genocidal outcomes.

These tendencies are *implicit* in the operational principles and outcomes of all zero sum games, and therefore in all hierarchical systems and structures, which are grounded in the following three fundamental "zero-sum" assumptions:

1. Resources are scarce and there are not enough to go around

2. It is therefore necessary to compete with one another for access to these resources, which directly impact the ability to survive and thrive

3. As a consequence, my/our gain requires your/their loss, and my/our victory requires your/their defeat

Non-zero-sum games, on the other hand, do not *require* competition, or a single universally acceptable solution, or an optimal strategy that is preferable to all others, or a fixed pie, or predictable outcomes, or a single truth, or anyone to lose so that others can win. Non-zero-sum games are cooperative or collaborative but may include competitive elements. Participants in non-zero-sum games often have complementary or overlapping interests but may have some that are opposed. In cooperative games, players are able to communicate, plan, and reach agreements in advance, while in competitive or non-cooperative games, except for the rules of the game, they are not. The operational principles and outcomes of non-zero sum games and all collaborative, *heterarchical* systems and structures, are grounded in three non-zero-sum assumptions:

1. Resources can be increased through collaboration, and shared so there are enough to go around

2. All players depend on one another for access to these resources, which directly impact everyone's ability to survive and thrive

3. As a consequence, by working together, we all gain and can cover one another's losses, so that my/our victory does not require your/their defeat

Participants in non-zero-sum games may have multiple diverse interests, values, and goals. Building on the work of mathematician John F. Nash (described in Sylvia Nasar's *A Beautiful Mind*), a utility function can therefore be used to assign a number to each separate interest, in order to convey its relative importance, priority, or attractiveness to each person or group. These interests do not need to be entirely "rational," and can have emotional or subjective components, such as a desire to help someone in need, or share in the proceeds or benefits, or punish a wrongdoer.

The more these interests overlap, the more advantageous communication, planning, consensus, collaboration, negotiation, and conflict resolution become; and the more complex, collaborative, higher order skills are required to succeed. Harvard professor Martin Novak has demonstrated that when people belong to a network, cooperation quickly becomes dominant over competition, especially when the benefit-to-cost ratio exceeds the average number of neighbors, and when long-term goals, community relations, and reputations for cooperation are taken into consideration.

Elinor Ostrom has gone further, earning the Nobel Prize in economics for research demonstrating that collaboration is the *best* process for diverse groups of people to use in working together and solving problems, where eight minimal conditions are met:

1. The group and its purpose are clearly defined
2. The costs and benefits are shared equally
3. Decisions are made by consensus
4. Misconduct is monitored
5. Sanctions start out mild and escalate only as needed
6. Conflict resolution is fast and fair
7. The group has the authority to manage its own affairs
8. The relationship of the group with others is appropriately structured

What is often missing in efforts to encourage the use of non-zero sum processes is widespread recognition that these higher order skills and capacities emerge when, and *as*, people are allowed to interact with each other in synergistic, caring, non-zero sum ways. People learn how to collaborate by participating in collaborative processes and relationships, in the course of which, diversity, dissent, and conflicts are encountered and overcome, allowing newer, higher forms of connection and resolution to arise.

How Zero-Sum Games Lead to Bias, Stereotyping, Prejudice, and Discrimination

The goal and outcome of every zero-sum game, especially in social, economic, political, or ecological settings, is the creation of a hierarchy of winners and losers, haves and have-nots, in-groups and out-groups, advantaged and disadvantaged, dominant and subordinate, superior and inferior, powerful and powerless. These hierarchical outcomes are then *fixed* as rigidly as possible by the winners in superficially neutral systems and structures, organizations and institutions, laws and adjudications, rules and regulations, policies, and procedures, so as to discourage "rank jumping" and minimize the frequency and impact of future conflicts over justice and fairness. They do so in part by making these aspirations appear unnecessary, unnatural, impossible, or pointless; in part by refusing to acknowledge the reality of mistreatment, or the history and impact of inequity; and in part by failing to recognize or admit the "prejudice of the middle," or, as Rebecca Solnit brilliantly suggests, the "bias of the status quo."

> The idea that all bias is some deviation from an unbiased center is itself a bias that prevents pundits, journalists, politicians, and plenty of others from recognizing some of the most ugly and impactful prejudices and assumptions of our times. I think of this bias, which insists the center is not biased, not afflicted with agendas, prejudices, and destructive misperceptions, as status-quo bias. Underlying it is the belief that things are pretty OK now, that the people in charge should be trusted because power confers legitimacy, that those who want sweeping change are too loud or demanding or unreasonable, and that we should just all get along without looking at the skeletons in the closet and the stuff swept under the rug. It's mostly a prejudice of people for whom the system is working, against those for whom it's not.

These widely accepted, seemingly legitimate, superficially neutral, yet status quo biased systems and structures then invite, permit, discount, and ignore *implicitly* hostile "private" communications and behaviors, stereotypes and slurs, biases and prejudices, ostracisms and discriminations, rationalizations, and defenses, each of which may be large or small, overt or covert, direct or subtle, personal or impersonal, violent or civil. Yet these communications and behaviors are clearly intended to intimidate and punish, coerce and control, and thereby preserve and consolidate a hierarchical ranking system that separates those who are privileged and offered easy access to status, wealth, power, and advantage from those who are not, those who belong and those who do not, and are denied membership in the club. By means of these distinctions and consolidations, race is converted into caste, gender into patriarchy, and wealth into class.

If our attention is *exclusively* concerned with overt expressions of prejudice at the interpersonal level of biased communications and behaviors, we will fail to recognize or address their covert, subtle, impersonal, and "civil" expressions; or the systems and structures that periodically trigger them; or the underlying assumptions, attitudes, and motivations that feed them; or the zero sum algorithms, operating systems, rules, and codes on which they are based, and from which they emerge.

What Connects All Forms of Prejudice?

Bias, stereotyping, prejudice, and discrimination, like the competitive, hierarchical, zero-sum assumptions on which they are based, are nearly universal, even *instinctual* responses to perceived competitors, antagonists, and opponents. We intuitively recognize that there are similarities between racism, sexism, classism, homophobia, xenophobia, anti-Semitism, Islamophobia, ageism, ableism, and all their countless hate-filled cousins. But what is it exactly that links them?

In the first place, each *specific* or "local" expression of bias, stereotyping, prejudice, and discrimination forms part of a *general*, or "global" effort to divide and segregate people for the purpose of placing them in one of three camps – those to whom we willingly give, those with whom we are willing to share, and those toward whom we feel justified in acting selfishly. In other words, those we place above us in status, wealth, power, and ecological advantage; those we regard as peers with equal status, and those we consider beneath us; those invited to the feast and sit at the table, those who serve and eat in the kitchen, and those who are kept outside and scavenge whatever remains.

Every stereotype and slur have the same derisive, adversarial, contemptuous common denominator: superiority over others. For this reason, they require us to reject not only empathy and compassion, but facts and logic, whether in science or art, law or politics, because only "alternate facts" and implicitly prejudiced conspiratorial theories permit the mind to operate irrationally and hostilely toward people we do not know and who have done us no harm, yet we would otherwise easily recognize as human and equal.

More critically for mediators, all biases, stereotypes, prejudices, and discriminations can be seen as steps, stages, elements, or components in the creation and escalation of every conflict. In the beginning, we may simply have preferences — perhaps regarding people, personalities, or behaviors, each grounded in our own needs and desires, pleasant or unpleasant associations, and personal histories; or in cognitive biases, cognitive ease, and familiarity. These are experienced as attraction, aversion, and "ordinary" biases.

Next, we may group people together based on some common characteristic we associate with personal advantage or disadvantage, pleasure or displeasure, approval or disapproval, agreement or disagreement, attraction or disgust, and *multiply* it based on our proximity, history, and rivalry; then multiply it *again* based on the emotional intensity of our fear, anger, jealousy, guilt, grief, or pain. We then simplify, rationalize, and consolidate these judgments by turning them into group stereotypes, based not on who other people actually *are*, but on what they *represent*, and arrange them in hierarchical order based on our relationship with those who share that characteristic.

Afterwards, we may *weaponize* these stereotypes by sharpening them into slurs and insults, using them to recruit allies, and turning them against a common enemy. We can then externalize our shame and guilt, feel superior, rationalize our selfishness, and more easily legitimize our inability to relate to others as equals. Next, we prejudge everything about them, in order to dismantle our capacity for empathy and compassion and suppress our awareness of what we have done. We then feel able to prejudge, discriminate, and dominate others, safeguard our privileges, and vindicate our unequal entitlement to status, wealth, power, and ecological advantage.

These steps, stages, elements, or components in the escalation of conflict help explain the *endurance* of bias, stereotyping, prejudice, and discrimination, and allow us to more readily recognize their role in all conflicts, in shaping the ways we think about and treat our opponents and blocking us from working together to solve our problems. We can then consider *all* conflict resolution processes, methods, and techniques to be potentially useful as generic responses to bias, stereotyping, prejudice, and discrimination.

For instance, it is common for mediators to design processes that encourage hostile and conflicted parties to agree on ground rules for their conversations; to clarify and agree on shared values; to engage in active listening, empathy building, power balancing, and dialogue; to acknowledge emotions, and surface interests; to identify appropriate criteria, brainstorm, and solve problems; to build consensus, negotiate collaboratively, and design conflict resolution systems. And each of these is a potentially useful way of reducing bias, stereotyping, prejudice, and discrimination.

These methods have proven successful in mediation in part because bias, stereotyping, prejudice, and discrimination are alive and well in every conflict. Do we not form biases against our opponents? Do we not stereotype, pre-judge, and discriminate against them? Indeed, the systems and structures that reinforce biased communications and behaviors are often simply large-scale expressions of small-scale conflict responses. Here is roughly how I think this happens, on both macro and micro scales.

When we are in conflict, it is incredibly time-consuming, unpleasant, and emotionally exhausting to interpret enormous amounts of important, potentially painful sensory data regarding many individuals piece-by-piece. As a result, our brains have learned to *approximate* the world by reducing complex, conflicting, noisy, upsetting, and ambiguous data from our senses, and turning them into simplistic, unitary, clear, emotionally acceptable, and unambiguous appraisals, opinions, groups, and judgments. This combination of massive amounts of unclear or unreliable data and an urgent need to act quickly, forces the brain to rely on rough guesswork, preconceived patterns, short-cuts, data compressions, simplifications, and heuristics – in other words, on *biases* and stereotypes, in an effort to make instantaneous sense of it all. These biases and stereotypes guide an iterative process, grounded in Bayesian logic, that *guesstimates* reality, rather than getting bogged down in attempting to accurately and reliably reproduce it, then (in theory) modifies its predictions as new information is received.

The difficulty arises from the fact that there are at least *two* sets of inputs that are automatically entered into every approximation: first, there is *objective* data that is derived from our senses; second, there are our *subjective* neurophysiological reactions and emotional responses to that data, which are triggered by our quick estimation of its subjective *meaning*, based on memories, associations, and degrees of sensitivity. Our interpretation of the meaning of what we sense not only prioritizes, organizes, and shapes the data, but selectively *distorts* it, creating "false positives" and "false negatives," in the form of answers that are convincing, yet demonstrably wrong. This process has been studied in great detail and forms the basis for Nobel Prize winner Daniel Kahneman's excellent description in *Thinking Fast and Slow,* and subsequent elaboration in *Noise,* with Olivier Sibony and Cass R. Sunstein.

Bias, Conflict, and Resolution

What is missing in Kahneman's, and most other accounts, is a full treatment of the role *conflict* plays in forming and sustaining biases, and the equally important role *conflict resolution* plays in dismantling and preventing them. Yet the most powerful cognitive biases are also "logical" responses to perceived conflicts that lead easily to "illogical" outcomes. For example, there is "confirmation bias," which is the tendency to believe data that confirms our beliefs and fulfills our expectations and disbelieve data that conflicts with them; or "reaction devaluation," which devalues proposals just because they originate with an adversary. There is even an explicit "zero sum heuristic," which intuitively judges situations to be zero sum whenever there is a conflict.

These ways of thinking directly connect bias with conflict, and therefore with conflict resolution, and as a result, we can conjecture: first, that all biases are aggravated and turned in a competitive, adversarial, hierarchical, zero sum direction by the experience of conflict; and second, that all biases are diminished and turned in a cooperative, collaborative, heterarchical, non-zero sum direction by the experience of resolution.

We can also conjecture that the methods used to resolve conflicts and end biased, stereotyped, prejudiced, or discriminatory communications and behaviors may succeed on an interpersonal level, yet *not* succeed at the level of systems and structures, or processes and relationships, or underlying zero sum attitudes and assumptions, and *vice versa*. Even the *language* that is appropriate and successful on one level may fail to find its mark or be heard as insulting or inappropriate when used at a different level.

The immediate, *short*-term goal of collaborative, interest-based approaches to bias and dispute resolution is then to discourage the use of destructive, adversarial, emotionally charged communications and behaviors. The *mid*-term goal is to shift from power- and rights- to interest-based systems and structures by strengthening support for diversity, dissent, dialogue, collaborative negotiation, restorative justice, mediation, and similar socially unifying processes. The *long*-term goal is to redesign the adversarial, chronically conflicted, hierarchical, zero-sum-based systems and structures, organizations and institutions, processes and relationships that invite biased, conflicted communications and behaviors, and the attitudes and assumptions that trigger them.

The combined *core* goal is therefore to ameliorate and prevent pointless, painful, and destructive conflicts at their chronic *source*, which can only be achieved by shifting from biased, conflicted, competitive, power- and rights-based, hierarchical, top-down, zero-sum, either/or, win/lose, "us versus them" attitudes and assumptions, processes and relationships, algorithms and operating systems; to unbiased, mediative, collaborative, interest-based, heterarchical, bottom-up and sideways, non-zero sum, both/and, win/win, "us versus it" ones.

Alternative Ways of Defining Bias, Stereotyping, Prejudice, and Discrimination

Reflecting on the language that defines the first, interpersonal level of communications and behaviors, it is useful to distinguish the various meanings, manifestations, forms, and purposes of "bias," or "stereotyping," or "prejudice," and "discrimination," which have many definitions, most of which are overlapping. Here are mine:

- *Bias* is preference, partiality, predisposition, or favoritism, as people may favor their left hand over their right, or facts that confirm what they already believe. Everyone has biases of multiple kinds, often based on cognitive ease, familiarity, priming, group affiliation, and identity.
- *Stereotyping* is lumping people together in groups based on a small subset of characteristics, giving them a shaming spin, and judging everyone in the group by those characteristics, whether they apply or not. (For more detailed definitions of stereotypes and slurs, see below.)
- *Prejudice* is pre-judgment, or deciding in advance based on biases and stereotypes, how positively or negatively we feel about those we identify as belonging to a group, and how we intend to associate with or relate to them, without regard for them as individuals, or who they actually are.
- *Discrimination* is the hostile, oppressive, and exploitative

marginalization, estrangement, ostracism, segregation, domination, suppression, and unequal treatment of people, based on biases, stereotypes, and prejudices.

Using these definitions, and considering them from the interest-based perspective of mediation, we can imagine any number of ways of thinking about and responding to incidents, allegations, and perceptions of bias, stereotyping, prejudice, and discrimination, and redefining them, depending on circumstances, alternatively as:

- Differences in how we respond to others depending on their membership in a caste, gender, class, or group, together with an inability or unwillingness to listen
- Unfair treatment based solely on group identity or appearance
- Language, attitudes, or behaviors that assume or assert dominance and superiority over others, or regard them as alien or "other"
- Negative stories and narratives about others that distance us from them
- Efforts to attain unequal status, wealth, power, or ecological advantage through bullying or shaming
- Self-hatred and negative self-esteem transferred onto others
- Unconscious use of cognitive biases, stereotypes, and "fast" thinking that bypass empathy and rational thought, and favor selfish and adversarial responses over sharing and collaborative ones
- Unconscious antagonistic responses to perceived loss of status, wealth, power, or ecological advantage
- Feelings of guilt, shame, or fear of retribution, retaliation, and reparation for past acts of prejudice, which have been reversed, transformed into arrogance, and attributed to others
- Rationalizations, excuses, and insincere explanations for hostile, adversarial, and disrespectful behavior toward others

- Efforts to diminish, reduce, subordinate, shame, or dehumanize others, perhaps as a projection of our own guilt or lack of self-confidence
- Unheard or unrecognized cries for help, requests for change, desires for a better relationship
- Methods for disarming empathy and compassion in preparation for harming others, and their replacement with arrogance, disrespect, and disgust
- Means of acquiring unequal social status, inequitable economic wealth, autocratic political power, or ecological advantage by taking them from others; or justifications for their unfair distribution
- Structures and systems, or processes and relationships, whether in couples, families, organizations, institutions, cultures, or societies, that routinely regenerate inequality, inequity, and autocracy

The value of imagining different ways of defining bias, stereotyping, prejudice, and discrimination, is that each may lead to a more finely tuned and advanced set of skills and responses than if we simply regard them as "bad behaviors," or "evil." It then becomes possible to identify a set of interest-based methods and approaches that lead to more successful conversations, dialogues, problem solving discussions, collaborative negotiations, mediations, restorative justice practices, and systems design efforts to redress and repair the problem on multiple levels, starting with stereotypes and slurs.

How to Create, Mediate, and Dismantle Stereotypes and Slurs

Stereotypes and slurs are the primary, practical, *specific* ways that systemic or structural biases, prejudices, and discriminations — and the *generic*, hierarchical, competitive, zero sum attitudes and intentions that give rise to them — manifest themselves at the interpersonal level of communications and behaviors. If we can identify and isolate the precise pieces, elements, components, and steps used to create them, we may then discover how to reverse, remove, and dismantle them piece-by-piece, depriving them of the key mechanisms or ingredients needed to successfully sow division. Here, for example, is a recipe or list of instructions on how to create a stereotype for any group:

1. Pick a characteristic
2. Blow it completely out of proportion
3. Reduce or collapse the whole person into the characteristic
4. Discount individual differences and variations
5. Disregard subtleties and complexities
6. Ignore our common humanity
7. Make it match our own worst fears
8. Make it shameful and cruel

It now becomes possible to successfully reverse and dismantle the stereotype, for example, by picking a different characteristic, reducing it to proportion, seeing the whole person as greater than the characteristic, accentuating individual differences, paying attention to subtleties and complexities, recognizing our common humanity, reducing fears, and encouraging self-confidence and kindness.

And, these are things mediators *routinely* do. Even at a simple level, if people in conflict stereotype each other and magnify their differences, mediators may reverse the stereotype and clarify their commonalities. Or if they are at impasse due to competitive, adversarial, win/lose assumptions, mediators may identify underlying interests that do not require competition, and explore collaborative, win/win outcomes.

The next *operational* step in the consolidation of bias, and its interpersonal expression as prejudice and discrimination, is the conversion of stereotypes into slurs and insults. Here is a set of generic instructions for inventing racial, gender, class, and similar slurs:

1. Identify the group as separate, distinct, alien, lesser, and "other"

2. Create truncated, humiliating, derogatory sounding names for the group

3. Distance oneself from members of the group, and encourage others to do the same

4. Withhold empathy and compassion from members of the group

5. De-legitimize and erode standards of reasonableness, fairness, and good faith in dealing with member of the group

6. Use "dog-whistle" humiliating euphemisms or "weasel words" about the group, while denying or even opposing the use of slurs

7. Express open contempt, derision, and disgust for the group

8. Justify bullying, dominance, and subordination over group members

9. Give implicit permission to rape, pillage, and harm group members

10. Introduce pre-genocidal slurs like "animals," "scum," and "filthy"

11. Impose living conditions that force people to live in ways that backwards justify the slur, and promote fear of contamination by contact

12. Get rid of the slur by getting rid of the people who have been labeled by it

Again, the value of breaking these and other prejudicial behaviors into smaller, distinct sub-parts is that each can be addressed separately using a variety of techniques, rather than relying on a single approach that may work in some cases but not in others. We can, for example, refuse to treat people who are different as though they were alien or lesser; or refuse to remain silent and countenance derogatory remarks directed at others; or decline to distance ourselves; or openly extend empathy, etc.

And again, mediators *routinely* disarm slurs and insults, for example, by identifying the interests that lie beneath them; or asking questions that surface them; or eliciting confessions of pain and vulnerability; or reframing the slur or insult. For example, a slur that describes someone as lazy can be reframed as a *confession* of feeling overworked and disrespected; or more deeply as a *request* to lend a hand, by asking questions that reveal these deeper underlying issues, such as:

- Do you feel you are being overworked?
- Do you feel the work has not been fairly divided? If so, how would you divide it?
- Do you feel disrespected when you are working hard and others are not helping out?
- What other words do you associate with the word "lazy"? Why?
- What life experiences have you had with people who are "lazy"?
- Are there any positive words you could use to describe someone who is lazy? What led you to use a negative word like "lazy" instead?
- Is there some part of you that would like to be lazy yourself? What are you afraid would happen if you were?
- Have you asked for help? If not, why not?
- Would you like to do so now?

In these ways, ordinary non-zero sum, interest-based mediation techniques offer a wide range of approaches that can be used to successfully dismantle stereotypes and slurs. And since the core components of prejudicial communications and behaviors are quite similar regardless of the group concerned, they can be dismantled in similar ways.

Shifting to Non-Zero-Sum Games

Thus, if we are to understand the power, endurance, and universality of bias, stereotyping, prejudice, and discrimination, we need to locate their sources not only in bigoted interpersonal communications and behaviors, or in skewed systems and structures, but in the competitive, hierarchical, zero-sum rubrics and algorithms that feed these chronically conflicted systems and structures, communications and behaviors, and are needed to sustain and support them.

Throughout human history, collaboration, sharing, and conflict resolution have proven extraordinarily successful, allowing us to band together and combine our diverse strengths and abilities in potent and creative ways, giving rise to extraordinary wealth and productivity. Yet history also proves the attractiveness of competition, selfishness, and adversarial attitudes toward conflict, which have led to staggering poverty, immense cruelty, and senseless destruction on increasingly unimaginable scales.

Conflict, competition, hierarchy, war, and zero-sum games have frequently prevailed, partly because they favor *personal* survival and reproduction, and partly because they require only lower order skills. On an interpersonal level, these conflicts take the form of insults, challenges to fight, and one-on-one battles, similar to the food and mating contests that occur in many other species. These aggressive, competitive, adversarial responses make sense as responses to competition for scarce resources and perceived conflicts of interest. Yet they also, in tightly knit, socially interdependent communities, result in devastating losses, unnecessary deaths, senseless destruction of resources, lingering resentments, deep distrust, loss of synergy, and chronic conflicts that weaken and divide the entire community, and sometimes the entire species, for decades.

As we increase in numbers; as our technology becomes exponentially more powerful; as we communicate more instantaneously; as we become more networked and connected; as we grow more socially, economically, politically, and ecologically interdependent; and as our destructive capacity continues to escalate, making nuclear and environmental annihilation easier to trigger, lower skilled adversarial outcomes begin to evaporate, and we are more and more compelled to learn higher order skills in collaboration, conflict resolution, and our responses to diversity and dissent.

Indeed, it is clear that our lives today consist *mostly*, and increasingly, of *non*-zero-sum games; that collaboration is *vastly* more productive and satisfying than competition; that hatred and domination significantly reduce morale and motivation in everyone (simply because no one wants to be hated or dominated); and that all of our conflicted social, economic, political, and ecological hierarchies; all our power-based pecking orders; and all the biases, stereotypes, prejudices, and discriminations we are directing at each other, are a *colossal* waste of human potential, resources, and time.

For these reasons, hyper-competitive, rigidly hierarchical win/lose processes *always* cost more than they benefit; generate unnecessary, chronic conflicts; and pit us against one another when we would be much better off uniting and facing our problems together. The differences between these opposing approaches are starkly highlighted in our varied responses to the Covid-19 pandemic, and in the cost in human lives of seeing it through biased, competitive, adversarial, politically polarized lenses.

We do not have to be passive recipients of adversarial rubrics and algorithms, or retributive, zero sum attitudes toward social justice. We can choose to change our conflicted, competitive, zero-sum algorithms, and the unspoken assumption that they must always end in hierarchies of winners and losers. In addition to adopting non-zero sum, collaborative, and mediative approaches to diversity and dissent, we can also:

1. Increase the number of "games," or processes in which many people are able to win — for example, by celebrating not only those who win a race, but those who enter it, those who assist others to complete it, those who hang in there to the end, and those who finish last

2. Base the hierarchies we are required to accept on shared values, ethical principles, and restorative ideas of justice and fairness — for example, by agreeing on ground rules for fair competition, and promoting circles, dialogues, collaborative negotiations, and respectful communications

3. Carefully limit the issues that depend on single truths, or that necessitate win / lose outcomes or winners and losers, by asking questions that have multiple correct answers; or by agreeing to refer *all* conflicts initially to informal problem solving, facilitated dialogue, collaborative negotiation, or mediation; or by reaching consensus on criteria, or priorities, or rubrics, or guidelines for triage — for example, by vaccinating the elderly first, or those who are most at risk of dying

4. Limit the impact of pecking orders and hierarchies by confining them to specific events and circumstances, and actively preventing them from expanding to others — for example, by ranking people according to their ability to perform a task and making sure that the ranking does not extend to unrelated areas or tasks

5. Enlarge the number of opportunities, dimensions, and arenas for people to advance in ranking — for example, by rewarding people for different kinds of learning, different skill sets, raising challenging issues, dissenting, promoting diversity, asking interesting questions, making the process more enjoyable, etc.

6. Increase the use of collaborative, heterarchical, non-zero sum processes *afterwards*, and help resolve chronic conflicts that get triggered by the use of competitive, hierarchical, zero sum ones — for example, by jointly evaluating what happened, and agreeing on ways of improving it

7. Shift the *culture* from one of conflict blame, punishment, and retributive justice to one of mediation, joint ownership, shared responsibility, and restorative justice — for example, by acknowledging the harm suffered by *everyone*, mediating disputes, and jointly seeking truth and reconciliation, and a return to community

8. Educate and train people in schools, workplaces, and communities in a wide range of non-zero-sum conflict resolution techniques; continually improve their skills, capacities, and readiness to use them; and help shift conflict

approaches from adversarial and avoidant, to collaborative and participatory ones – for example, by including dialogue facilitation, conflict coaching, circles, restorative justice, and conflict resolution skills as core curricula from kindergarten through college

Toward a Unified and Diverse, *Transformational* Response to Prejudice

What is missing in most of our responses to bias, stereotyping, prejudice, and discrimination is agreement on a unified yet diverse, global yet local, synchronized yet multi-faceted, transformational yet incremental approach; one that links each specific incident of bias to all the others, revealing their deeper interconnections, and showing how readily and easily they flow from one into another. Doing so will allow us to link arms and prevent us from pitting one ill-treated group against another in an often unspoken competition for sympathy, funding, and support. It will enable us to address problems on multiple levels, and in more than one way. It will help shift our approach from each group separately defending its own, to everyone defending each other.

Otherwise, we turn our backs and pay little or no attention as one form of prejudice seamlessly morphs into another, attacks a different group that looks less defended, retreats and seeks cover, denies it ever existed, adopts covert tactics, invents new euphemisms, switches forms, wraps itself in patriotism, and returns when some fresh crisis or conflict invites it, attacking whoever is weakest, and permitting competitive, hierarchical, adversarial, zero sum dynamics to reestablish the pecking order.

Yet even in these moments, our refusal to accept ostracism and dehumanization, superiority and domination, exploitation and oppression; our gifts of kindness and humanity, of solidarity with the damned, defamed, and despised; our clear and conscious linking of all the sundry stereotypes, slurs, insults, and forms of bias; our use of dialogue, mediation, and restorative justice practices to extend empathy, caring, and community to victims and perpetrators alike, can make an enormous difference.

While doing so will not be easy, on a small scale, these shifts are the essence and aim of every mediation, which invites adversaries to notice and dismantle the destructive biases, stereotypes, prejudices, and discriminations that prevent them from seeing each other as human beings, or as caring partners in creating collaborative communities and solving common problems.

This transformational shift from *retributive* forms of justice, which impose jail time, fines, and humiliating punishments for hate crimes; to *restorative* forms of justice, which seek apology, forgiveness, redemption, rehabilitation, reconciliation, and return to community for all, using mediation, dialogue, storytelling, empathy building, problem solving, restitution, and truth telling, offer us opportunities to dramatically reduce bias, stereotyping, prejudice, and discrimination by dismantling them finally in people's hearts and minds, i.e., in the smallest, least accessible, most guarded, and last places they are to be found.

There is beauty in all races. There is love in all genders. There is wealth in all classes. There is wisdom in all religions. There is poetry in all languages. There is caring in all countries. So why diminish or denigrate any when we can benefit from all? The famous cellist Pablo Casals asked a similar question: "The love of one's country is a splendid thing, but why should it stop at the border." Love, community, and what matters most in life, are not zero-sum games, and there is no need for them to stop anywhere.

TRANSFORMING CONFLICT CULTURES THROUGH MEDIATION

This chapter was written in an effort to better understand the role of culture in conflict resolution, and the possibilities for transformation. It will be published in 2022 in Dominic Busch's book, The Rotledge Handbook of Intercultural Mediation.

The choice of a point of view is the initial act of a culture.

— JOSE ORTEGA Y GASSET

If we are to achieve a rich culture, rich in contrasting values, we must recognize the whole gamut of human potentialities, and so weave a less arbitrary social fabric, one in which each diverse human gift will find a fitting place.

— MARGARET MEAD

Culture eats strategy for breakfast.

— PETER DRUCKER

We experience, engage in, resolve, transform, and transcend conflicts in three fundamental locations, arenas, or "fields," each with its own characteristics, rules, processes, algorithms, and dynamics:

1. *Internally* or personally, as sensory perceptions, neurophysiological responses, mental activities, emotional reactions, heartfelt desires, qualities of energy, and spiritual states that happen *inside* us
2. *Relationally* or socially, as active and passive communications, responsive behaviors, relationships, and interactions with others that take place *between* us
3. *Environmentally* or systemically, as cultures and contexts, rites and rituals, customs and practices, systems and structures that take place in couples and families, organizations and institutions, nations, and societies; along with the backdrops and settings, histories and experiences, economic and political conditions, ethics and values, and countless other circumstances that occur *around* us

Each of these interacts in complex, subtle, and intricate ways with the others. Each is a potential source of resistance and resolution, intractability and insight, revenge and reconciliation, instigation and prevention, retributive and restorative justice, stasis, and transformation. None is conflict neutral. Each contributes, often in veiled and unspoken, yet powerful ways to the nature, intensity, duration, impact, and meaning of our conflicts. Each *profoundly* impacts the quality of our lives, our personal capacity for joy and compassion, and our ability to collaborate in solving common problems.

Yet nearly all our attention in mediation is directed at its social or relational aspects, with comparatively little to its internal emotional, spiritual, and heartfelt aspects, and nearly none to its cultural, environmental, and systemic aspects. Why is this, why is it important, and what can be done to improve our ability to transform and enhance our conflict cultures?

What is Culture, and How Does it Generate Conflict?

There are dozens of ways of defining culture, most of which focus on customs, norms, social behaviors, beliefs, arts, and learning. Broadly, culture is how we approach our environment, how we group and separate from one another, how food is produced and consumed, how gender is perceived and displayed, how space and boundaries are established, how time is defined and used, how learning takes place, how people play and laugh, how goods are made, used, exchanged, and distributed.

Culture is how we perceive and process reality. It is shared beliefs, attitudes, behaviors, and customs. It is a way of life, a method for differentiating and integrating, a set of lessons on how to satisfy needs and navigate environments. It is an accumulation of successful adaptations, and agreed upon *meanings* of symbols, events, sensations, behaviors, and communications. It is what everyone knows, and no one talks about.

Culture is shaped beneath the surface, at a level deeper than conscious attention, where we seek to avoid the uncertainty and chaos of conflict; to alleviate, resolve, and learn from the fear and pain they provoke; to encourage cohesion, collaboration, and community — all of which require *significant* conflict resolution skills.

Families, groups, organizations, communities, and nations create cultures that draw people together despite their diversity, yet also discriminate against them based on their differences, discouraging disobedience, and punishing dissent. Most cultures create stories or narratives that describe how people should and should not behave, how they get into conflicts, with whom, over what, how they get resolved, and what happens when they don't.

Most importantly for mediators, culture is a way of assigning *meaning*, and every conflict happens partly because people assign different meanings to what was said and done, or not said and done. It is therefore axiomatic that *every* conflict is, on some level, cross-cultural. As the meaning of our conflicts is most important to us; and as every unique meaning alters the *form* of our conflict, creating fresh meanings, openings, insights, and approaches, cultural methods in mediation can trigger transformation, transcendence, prevention, and restorative outcomes.

How Cultures Assign Meaning

Cultural anthropologist, Edward T. Hall outlined the most important elements of culture in his classic book, *The Silent Language*, which he saw as creating rules for clarifying meaning — not only in interacting with the environment, but associating with others, assessing biases, competing, and collaborating for sustenance, navigating space and time, learning and playing, using property and fighting over it.

According to Hall, culturally defined meanings are *evolutionary* tools for transmitting messages. Space, for example, is a consequence of an animal's instinctive defense of its' lair, reflected in human society in office workers' defense of their cubicles, or fences around a home. Distinctions can be drawn between cultures in relation to their perceptions of space, for example, as closed vs. open, functional vs. aesthetic, separation vs. connection, empty vs. filled, thing vs. relationship, personal vs. social, face-to-face vs. side-by-side.

Similarly, contrasting meanings of time can give rise to conflicts, for example, as limited vs. unlimited, mono-chronic vs. poly-chronic, linear vs. circular, logical vs. emotional, being on time vs. being in time, time as money vs. time as sacred, controlled by schedule vs. flexible schedules, unitary vs. flowing. Conflicts commonly arise over other cultural issues, for example:

- Precision vs. ambiguity in communication
- Open vs. closed in personal information
- Verbal vs. written as a basis for traditions
- High vs. low context in establishing meaning

- Consensus vs. individualistic in decision making
- Formal vs. informal in processes
- Competitive vs. collaborative in relationships
- Direct vs. indirect in giving feedback
- Authoritarian vs. democratic in organization
- Deference vs. rebelliousness in relation to authority
- Exclusive vs. inclusive in relation to outsiders
- Linear vs. non-linear emphasis in thinking
- Gestalt vs. detail in orientation
- Appropriateness vs. inappropriateness in humor and play
- Demonstrative vs. restrained in emotional expression
- Permissive vs. directive in child rearing
- Fixed vs. fluid attitudes toward rules
- Open vs. closed attitudes toward outsiders
- Individual vs. group orientation in norms and values
- Interests vs. power or rights orientation in dispute resolution

Any of these can trigger conflicts that are mistaken, camouflaged, or superficially interpreted as "personality differences," yet can only be fully understood, resolved, and transformed by identifying their deeper cultural origins and collaboratively negotiating expectations for how they will be handled.

If we ask which of these conflicting cultural approaches is correct, it is clear that they are *all* correct, depending on context or circumstance. Therefore, collaborative, pluralistic *mediative* approaches to cultural diversity will predictably generate more complex, socially successful solutions to a wider range of problems than simpler, unitary ones.

We can also predict that conflict avoidant and highly competitive cultures will only be able to solve simple problems; and that collaborative cultures and advanced conflict resolution skills will increasingly be required as societies evolve and problems become more complex. This will happen because chronic cultural conflicts produce two fundamentally opposite outcomes:

1. Exclusive, competitive, hierarchical, "zero sum," power- or rights-based, coercion-driven approaches in which one side wins and the other loses, and the dispute resolution process *itself* eliminates much of the complexity and collaboration needed to fully solve problems, causing them to turn chronic

2. Synergistic, collaborative, heterarchical, non-zero sum, interest-based, consensus-driven approaches in which diverse cultures communicate and engage in dialogue with each other in a search for collaborative, synergistic solutions that are *at least* as complex and diverse as the problems they need to solve

Context, Culture, and the Attribution of Meaning in Conflict

In the everyday, unspoken give-and-take of diverse, conflicted human relationships, the "silent language" of culture plays a critical role. Edward T. Hall analyzed the ways people "talk" to one another without words, showing, for example, how the pecking order in a chicken yard is reflected in competition on a school playground or hierarchies at work. One of the ways cultures assign meaning is through "high and low context" communications, in which meaning depends on the amount of context needed to accurately interpret what is said. If, for example, we regard law as a culture consisting of precise definitions, little or no context is required to elucidate their meaning.

Emotional, romantic, and sexual communications, on the other hand, are subtle, nuanced, imprecise, and highly dependent on context to accurately assess the meaning of any behavior or statement. Even the word "hello" can be said in romantic, lewd, angry, curious, wistful, or happy ways. How, then, do we *know* what "hello" means? The answer depends on a set of cultural rules for turning context into meaning, *especially* the context of conflict, which requires *enormous* amounts of context to identify its meaning. This is why mediators need to be skilled in active listening, empathy, reframing, facilitated dialogue, nonviolent communication, appreciative inquiry, and similar methods; and able to elicit the parties' unique conflict cultures, including how each signals what things actually mean to them.

For these reasons, the resolution of any conflict is *necessarily* an act of culture. Indeed, if we look closely at the role played by culture in conflict, we can see that *every* conflict takes place in a rich cultural environment with myriad contextual elements that directly impact efforts to resolve it. Yet it is rare that mediators are trained in reading cultural contexts, or *"cultural intelligence,"* which consists partly of *interest-based* skills that aid us in:

1. Recognizing, categorizing, surfacing, exploring, and deepening people's understanding of their "conflict cultures," and how they can obstruct or improve their capacity for empathy and collaboration, and make agreements more arduous or easy
2. Revealing and dismantling the sources of cultural bias, stereotyping, prejudice, and discrimination through facilitated dialogue, culturally informed conversations, and advanced bias awareness and prejudice reduction techniques
3. Assisting conflicted parties in clarifying the contexts that create meaning for them and collaboratively negotiating the cultural norms and expectations they want to live by in their relationship with each other
4. Identifying guidelines for *designing* cultural approaches to conflict resolution that are creative, collaborative, and grounded in otherwise unspoken interests and understandings
5. Encouraging and promoting transformation and transcendence in conflict cultures, by redefining approaches to conflict in ways that deepen understanding and restorative outcomes

24 Ideas on Culture and Mediation

In implementing these skills in mediation, it is important to understand the roles cultures play in creating and resolving conflicts.

Here is a summary of 24 generic ideas, lessons, and insights that have been useful to me in conducting cross-cultural mediations and dialogues in many countries and communities over several decades:

1. Everyone creates culture — every person, family, age group, and organization — partly through stories that re-imagine and re-interpret life experiences.
2. Culture is what people understand without having to define or specify. It is the subtle, often unspoken ways of understanding and living in the world.
3. Culture includes the ways people set expectations, how they meet needs, what they imagine, how they relate to one another, what they do and do not react to, and how they react when they differ.
4. Cultures are largely defined by their differences from other cultures — the greater the difference, the more defined the culture.
5. Culture pre-determines what and how we see, hear, think, and feel. Whatever conflicts with our cultural assumptions are less accurately received and understood.
6. Most cultures assume they are superior to other cultures, and their ways are "right" or "better."
7. Conversely, opposing cultures are often seen as "wrong," or "inferior," and are judged, ridiculed, or insulted.
8. Most cultures value conformity, reward compliance, and punish dissent.
9. All cultures "socialize" their members, teaching them the "rules" and pressuring them to conform.
10. Among the teaching devices cultures use to socialize their members are myths about heroes and villains, parables about behaviors and consequences, metaphors for processing information, masks for defining the self, stereotypes, stories about conflict, narratives about people and groups, and "scripts" for all occasions.
11. Tolerance and acceptance of diversity and dissent within a

culture decrease as conflicts with other cultures increase and increase as conflicts with others decrease.

12. No culture is innately "better" or superior to any other. Each is capable of learning from others.

13. In *every* culture, people want to be accepted, listened to, acknowledged, and respected.

14. Cultural differences help define us, encourage positive values, and are reasons for celebration rather than fear.

15. All cultures have evolved methods for resolving conflicts and mediating differences, as well as sources of impasse and obstacles to resolution.

16. Cross-cultural conflicts arise even between members of the same culture, representing cracks in the culture, which are opportunities for adaptation, evolution, and improvement.

17. There are no absolute, universal "correct" responses to conflict, only *relatively* "right" or "wrong" ones within a given culture.

18. Not every conflict between people who are different is based on cultural differences.

19. We can't know all things about all cultures.

20. There are no universal problem solving, mediation, or conflict resolution techniques, processes, or methodologies that are successful always, everywhere, in all cultures and conditions.

21. In every culture, people want to be understood, and respond favorably to curiosity and respectful communication.

22. Cultural conflicts do not disappear when we ignore them.

23. There is ambiguity in diversity. Tolerance for diversity and keeping an open mind are therefore essential skills in mediating cross-cultural conflicts.

24. Cross-cultural collaboration improves through empathy and honesty, open dialogue, committed listening, integrity, and willingness to improve over time.

25 Techniques for Mediating Cross-Cultural Conflicts

In mediating cross-cultural conflicts, it is helpful to adopt an *attitude* of curiosity, genuine caring, empathy, honesty, and commitment to respectful and transparent communications, processes, and relationships. As mediators, we want to ask questions that reveal the hidden contexts, silent languages, unspoken expectations, and implicit cultural assumptions beneath the veneer of contested issues. Instead of defining culture as something "everyone knows and no one talks about," we re-define it as something everyone talks about, to discover what each person means.

Here are 25 generic exercises, activities, questions, and techniques based on my experience conducting cross-cultural mediations, bias awareness and prejudice reduction workshops, public dialogues, and cross-cultural conversations:

1. Co-mediate in culturally diverse teams.

2. Ask people what they expect of the process, who they think *you* are, and what role they would like you to play.

3. Invite each party to suggest someone from their culture to act as a process observer, to offer feedback during and after the session.

4. Establish common backgrounds, points of reference, and values for the process, for example, regarding the importance of cooperation, family, friendship, or education, then connect these to the issues.

5. Ask questions that elicit the role of culture in their conflict, for example:

- "What words do you use to describe the various kinds of conflict." "What do people typically do in each case?"
- "What is the meaning in your culture, for example, of crime? Silence? Public criticism? Physical contact? Yelling? Confidentiality? Use of first names? Mediation?"
- "How are conflicts typically handled in your culture, for example, between insiders and outsiders? Younger and

older? Women and men? Siblings? Employer and employee? Neighbors?"

- "How are emotions expressed and communicated in your culture." "Which are encouraged or discouraged?" "Why?"
- "How are mediations and negotiations typically conducted in your culture in relation to, for example, the role of the mediator? Aggressive or collaborative in style? Communication of emotions, 'bottom lines,' or hidden agendas? Role of outsiders? Compromise."

6. Ask questions like: "What does that mean to you?" "What does the word '_____' mean in your culture?" Record agreed-upon meanings for later reference.

7. Periodically ask, especially when discussions get difficult, "What can I/we do to make this process work better for you?"

8. Elicit a hierarchy of conflicts by identifying which are most serious and which are least, compare similarities and differences, and do the same with conflict styles.

9. Ask parties to rank the options for resolution in their culture from war to surrender, elaborate those that lie in the middle, and explore reasons for choosing collaborative approaches.

10. Ask them to state, pantomime, role-play, draw, or script how conflicts are commonly handled in their cultures.

11. Ask them to list *positive* words that describe the other party's culture, and alongside, positive words that describe their own, then exchange lists and compare them, pointing out similarities and differences in perceptions.

12. Consider conducting the same exercise more dangerously by eliciting *negative* words and stereotypes regarding their own culture, then searching for neutral or positive words that reframe them and discuss.

13. Surface, acknowledge, and model respect for cultural differences by asking people if they are proud of their culture. If so, why, and if not, why not.

14. Or, more dangerously, consider asking if there is anything they *dislike* about their culture, and why.

15. Ask them to describe a stereotype others have of their culture, say whether they think it applies, and why or why not.

16. Ask each person to describe the heroes, victims, villains, mediators, or others in their culture, then compare and contrast them.

17. Ask them to describe the most important lessons they learned from their culture, who taught them, why they were important, and how they might be used to resolve this dispute.

18. Ask them to bring photographs of their families, the homes they grew up in, or themselves as children, share these with each other, and describe three crucible events that made them who they are today.

19. Ask each party to write about the conflict as a story or fable, using neutral names and a third-person voice, perhaps starting with "Once upon a time ..." and ending with "and they all lived happily ever after," then read them aloud to each other.

20. As the mediator, describe your *own* culture, the stereotypes others have of it, the stereotypes you were taught about your own or other cultures, and how you overcame them.

21. Create an appreciation of culture by asking what they would miss most if it disappeared.

22. Jointly design a consensus-based cross-cultural model for conflict prevention, resolution, transformation, and reconciliation.

23. Ask for honest feedback about how you did as mediator, and how you might do better next time.

24. Ask one thing each person learned, will do differently, or will take away from the mediation.

25. Ask each person to bring a song, dance, poem, ritual, work of art, food, etc. from their culture to the next mediation, break bread, and jointly celebrate your work together.

We can also ask people to meet in small groups and brainstorm elements of the "old culture," what elements they would like to include in the "new culture," and three to five ways of expressing them; or suggestions for how the mediators can encourage collaborative outcomes; or elements they would like to add to their culture to strengthen its mediative capacities.

In intractable and hostile disputes, we can target ways of assigning meaning by asking questions that elicit cultural filters and lenses. For example, in the midst of an argument, we can ask: "What do you think is the meaning of what she just said?" "Why do you think that is what she meant." "Do you think she agrees with your understanding of what she meant?" "Would you like to find out." "Why don't you ask her right now." Or during a hostile exchange, we can ask, "Excuse me, is this conversation working." "Why not?" "What is one thing the other person can do that would make it work better for you?" "Are you willing to do that, starting now."

How to Transform Conflict Cultures in Mediation — Two Examples

Because cultures are partly *imagined*, they can be re-imagined. Because they are open, malleable, regenerative, and plastic, they can be reshaped in mediation. Here are two examples of deep, profound, simple, yet transformational changes that took place through a culturally informed mediation processes.

Example one. Several years ago, I was asked to mediate nearly a dozen conflicts between doctors and nurses at a children's hospital. After conducting several interviews, it became clear that the hospital was a highly stressed, *chronically* conflicted cultural environment in which everyone was working long hours, children were dying and being saved, and there was no acknowledgement or support for a completely exhausted and massively burned-out staff.

Instead of mediating on a "triaged," case-by-case basis, I brought the staff together to report on what I found. I said we were not genies but would like each person to offer one wish for how they might create a less stressful work environment. A nurse said he gave everything he had every week to the children who were his patients, and he wished that at the end of the week, someone would give him a flower, as a way of recognizing his efforts. This impressed me as a powerful suggestion, so I asked him, "Would you be willing to start, and give flowers to the people you work with." He said he would, and I asked everyone else, "Raise your hand if you are willing to join him." Every hand went up. Within a week, every Friday, the hospital was *filled* with flowers.

The next person who spoke suggested creating a tone over the loudspeaker to mark every time a child died, so everyone could stop, just for a second, to say goodbye to that child; plus a different tone to mark every time a child's life was saved, so everyone could stop for a second to celebrate what they had achieved. In these small, seemingly insignificant ways, the *entire culture* of the hospital was transformed overnight, conflicts dramatically dropped in numbers and severity, morale improved significantly, stress declined, and people realized they could collaboratively re-imagine and transform their conflict culture.

Example two. In a different case, I was asked to help *prevent* conflicts that were about to emerge in a cardboard box factory that was in a dilapidated, unpainted, concrete block building in a dirt lot that became muddy whenever it rained. The manager was an elderly Latino man who had been promoted from the ranks and was now retiring and being replaced by a younger Anglo woman being brought in from the outside. The workers were all middle-aged Latino men who the owners knew would resent and rebel against the new manager, creating costly, demoralizing conflicts.

I met with the new manager, and we came up with a plan. On the weekend before her first day at work, she, her husband and two sons painted the factory inside and out, built a concrete walkway so no one had to walk through the dirt and mud, and planted flowers at the entrance. She put lace curtains on the windows, rugs on the floor, and paintings on the walls. She brought comfortable chairs for them to sit in, a coffee maker, small refrigerator and microwave, table and chairs to eat at, nice plates and cups for everyone, and a CD player to play their favorite music. When the workers arrived on Monday morning, she was there to greet them each by name, and they were utterly stunned by what she had done. They felt so deeply respected and acknowledged by her that for a long time there were *zero* conflicts.

By fundamentally transforming the culture of the factory, she made it harder for them to behave rudely, even in conflict, simply by putting lace curtains on the windows, rugs on the floors, paintings on the walls, soft chairs to sit in, coffee to drink, a table to sit and break bread at, and pleasant music to play.

In both examples, chronic conflicts were triggered less by high conflict personalities, disrespectful communications, and hostile behaviors than by stressful uncaring, disrespectful cultures, whose meanings could be negated by *proactively* identifying contrary meanings, then redesigning the environment and culture to express them.

Creating Cultural Maps in Mediation

Culture is a kind of *map* that teaches people how to navigate their conflicts, and mediation can help them figure out what to do when they get lost or disoriented, or changes take place that alter the meaning of previously understood symbols and directions. We can get confused and move off course in any of the locations of conflict, especially when the map itself is changing. As philosopher William Irwin Thompson described it,

A culture provides an individual with a mapping of time and space, but as the culture goes through a period of change and stressful transformation, this map becomes distorted. In periods of intense cultural distortion, the map becomes so changed as to be almost obliterated. For some this can be a moment of terror, for others, a time of release... The old forms fall away, there comes a new receptivity, a new centering inward, and in an instant there flashes onto the screen of consciousness a new re-visioning of the map.... [N]ew possibilities of time and space announce themselves, possibilities that lie beyond the descriptions of the old institutions of the old culture. This is the prophetic moment, the annunciation of a new myth, and the beginning of a new culture.

Mediation can assist people in becoming more aware of the ways their culture maps alternate paths through conflict and design new, *combined* maps that enable them to more successfully navigate their disputes, and to resolve, forgive, reconcile, and prevent them — not only internally and relationally, but culturally, systemically, and environmentally as well.

Cultural maps, unlike ancient atlases, are less depictions of what is known than cautionary tales, secret codes, cryptic guides, pious sentiments, moral rationalizations, and justifications for failure. To map conflicts in *transformational* ways, we need to "cultivate" cultures that are less avoidant, accommodating, and adversarial, and more collaborative, consensus-based, and mediative; cultures that actively encourage diversity and dissent, dialogue and negotiation, mediation and restorative justice.

We need to strengthen the elements within our cultures that *discourage* bias and prejudice, conditioned passivity and reactiveness, hyper-competition and selfishness, cynicism and apathy, shaming and blaming, manipulation and demagoguery, stories of victimization and demonization, dependence on hierarchy and external authority, blind obedience and acceptance of covert behaviors, defenses against empathy and lack of ownership of "someone else's problem." And *all* of these are natural, transformational attributes of the culture of mediation.

Last, it is essential for mediators to appreciate that *culture* is intimately connected — not only to the *content* of conflict and meaning of the issues, but to its *processes* and *relationships*, as well. Indeed, every genuine transformation in mediation necessarily shifts all four aspects, strengthening them at their core, and generating a multi-dimensional map that allows us to transform and transcend conflicts in all these areas.

By doing so, we discover and design pioneering approaches that *invite* us to evolve to higher orders of conflict and resolution; to invent new maps, avert future conflicts, and restore justice and community to people who have been alienated from one another, which are the highest, most heartfelt, transformative and *transcendent* purposes of every conflict culture.

19

MEDIATION AND THE EVOLUTION OF DEMOCRACY:

INVENTING INTEREST-BASED RESPONSES TO LYING, DEMAGOGUERY, AND FASCIS

[I]t was impossible to have a proper grasp of humanitarianism, culture, and democracy if one endorsed [the Nazi] conception, or to be more precise misconception, of heroism.

— VICTOR KLEMPERER

One kind of propaganda, demagogic speech, both exploits and spreads flawed ideologies. Hence, demagogic speech threatens democratic deliberation. A different kind of propaganda, civic rhetoric, can repair flawed ideologies, potentially restoring the possibility of self-knowledge and democratic deliberation.

— JASON STANLEY

[W]e were not strong, only aggressive; we were not free, merely licensed; we were not compassionate, we were polite; not good, but well behaved. We courted death in order to call ourselves brave, and hid like thieves from life. We substituted good grammar for intellect; we switched habits to simulate maturity; we rearranged lies and called it truth ...

— TONI MORRISON

Many political conflicts can be resolved by skillfully applying a combination of fairly straightforward informal problem solving, dialogue, consensus building, conflict coaching, collaborative negotiation, group facilitation, mediation, and similar interest-based conflict resolution methods and techniques.

More difficult issues arise, however, when political conflicts deepen and fester, leading people to blatantly and consistently lie; to act demagogically and aggressively; or to behave fascistically, in the sense of being committed to hostile, win/lose contests against enemies who have been pre-defined as sub-human, unworthy of respect, and legitimate to brutalize or kill.

As in all conflict resolution efforts, it is important to learn from the most difficult cases, which can lead to insights that improve our ability to resolve far less onerous problems. To begin, we need to consider how and why lying, demagogic, adversarial, and fascistic behaviors arise in political conflicts, and what we can do to minimize them — if possible, without slipping into equally adversarial, win/lose behaviors that provide them with backwards justification.

The Fragility of Electoral Democracies

Nearly 2500 years ago, Plato warned that, "Dictatorship naturally arises out of democracy, and the most aggravated form of tyranny and slavery out of the most extreme liberty." Why should this be the case? In mediation terms, and with the benefit of hindsight, we can say that an initial difficulty emerges out of the organization of *electoral* democracies as rights-based, competitive, adversarial, zero-sum games in which vast amounts of status, wealth, and power are won or lost based on win/lose public contests for political office.

It is routinely declared and publicly maintained, even by the most corrupt and autocratic regimes, that their electoral contests are governed by fair procedures according to universal rules that are legally binding and neutrally enforced. Yet this declaration, even if true, leaves open the possibility that anyone sufficiently corrupt or ruthless will decide to "stack the deck" and pretend to follow the rules, while subverting their clear and obvious intent for personal or partisan gain. As Plato viewed it,

> Democracy, by permitting freedom of speech, opens the door for a demagogue to exploit the people's need for a strongman; the strongman will use this freedom to prey on the people's resentments and fears. Once the strongman seizes power, he will end democracy, replacing it with tyranny ...

While we may disagree with Plato's conflation of democracy with anarchy, and his belief that freedom of speech is to blame for tyranny, his critique reveals a deeper, far more subtle, yet fatal flaw that lies at the heart of every "rights-based" legal standard, judicial process, and constitutional guarantee. Each of these depends ultimately, and from time to time *entirely*, on the willingness of elected and appointed officials — not only to create laws and rules that are fair and the same for everyone — but to follow them, neutrally enforce them, and risk their lives and careers by being willing to stand up for them. And in times of crisis, they are required to do so *against* the wishes of people with far greater status, wealth, and power; people who are determined to resort to lying, bullying, bribery, coercion, contempt, and a variety of legal and illegal means, including violence, to retain them.

The combination of open, fragile, rights-based electoral democracies with episodic crises caused by chronic, unresolved conflicts over social inequality, economic inequity, and political autocracy — or rather, the combination of deeply divided, unequal, and chronically conflicted societies with hierarchical, zero sum approaches to allocating resources and addressing problems — *automatically* generates, in the deepest crises, desperate attempts to circumvent the rules so as not to lose — both by those at the top and those at the bottom, as each recognizes that elections are always decided by majority rule, and will therefore naturally tend to favor the people and policies that occupy the middle.

In extreme circumstances, these crises and conflicts give rise to a widespread willingness to sacrifice democracy itself; but more commonly, to skew the electoral system *by design* so as to routinely produce results that favor the dominant, wealthy, and powerful. This is increasingly done not only by crass methods like ballot stuffing, but by more subtle techniques, like:

- Restricting the franchise, i.e., to citizens, property owners, non-slaves, males, adults, those who are literate, etc.
- Raising the cost of running for office so that only the wealthy can afford to run
- Cutting restrictions on campaign contributions by corporations and wealthy donors
- Establishing "winner-take-all" elections that selectively reward large, coalition-based parties and middle-of-the-road candidates who compromise and take centrist positions, resulting in "duopolopies" that rotate being in power
- Sidelining small independent parties and candidates
- Permitting those already in office to revise the rules and reshape them to favor their reelection
- Gerrymandering districts to make sure there is a majority who favor the party in power and minorities are under-represented
- Removing mailboxes and mail sorting machines, reducing staff, and defunding or shutting down parts of the postal service to block mail-in balloting
- Interfering with the census count in order to shift representation to less populous and more conservative states

- Closing polling places in neighborhoods likely to vote for the "wrong" candidate
- Placing obstacles in the way of voting, like poll taxes, literacy tests, voter ID cards, restrictions on mail-in ballots, restricting voting hours, etc. in order to selectively discourage those who might vote for the other party

More shrewdly, it is possible to swing the entire *culture* of politics in a simplistic direction by reducing it to contests over ego, personality, charisma, fame, seductiveness, slickness, and charm, while at the same time endeavoring to conceal, obscure, and publicly lament their *inseparable* dark side, consisting of personal attacks, egomania, bullying, gas-lighting, manipulation, pretense, duplicity, betrayal, and corruption.

Together, these methods convert the state and the entire political process into a spectacle, a charade, a televised reality show, an attribute of personal power. These lead to the creation of an apolitical, media-dominated culture that sidelines citizens, provokes controversy, and ignores, trivializes, or sensationalizes repeated incidents of phoniness, amorality, addictive behavior, pretense, deception, disgrace, cover-ups, lies, and scandals committed by its leaders.

L'État, C'Est Moi

An important element in the rise of lying, demagoguery, and fascism arises from what Harold Lasswell referred to as "the psychopathology of politics." Many observers have made the connection between egotistical, self-serving, demagogic, dictatorial, fascistic styles of leadership, and lying, narcissistic, sociopathic, aggressive, antagonistic, bullying behaviors, but few have recognized the ways these behaviors emerge *naturally* and inevitably as a consequence of zero-sum political games.

Once any process has been defined in win/lose terms, if the stakes are high enough, the rest happens somewhat automatically, in more or less the following way: if there is a single truth, a single correct path forward, a single solution to any problem and it is exclusively *mine*, the only remaining question is: what am I willing to do to suppress those who favor an opposing truth, path, or solution, in order to dominate the process and control the outcome?

Lying, narcissism, sociopathy, aggression, antagonism, and bullying are then able to produce successful outcomes, in the form of victories over less ruthless and more honest or scrupulous opponents. These behaviors therefore emerge naturally and effortlessly from zero sum assumptions, reaching their limit in the demagogic, dictatorial, and fascistic politics that always arise and receive mass support during periods of intractable conflicts, rapid changes, and systemic crises.

These behaviors result in short-term "victories," or successes when problems actually are simple, one-sided, frightening, or urgent; or when important resources are scarce and competition is rife; or when conflicts become violent, highly polarized, and seemingly intractable. Yet each victory entails someone else's defeat; each success spells another person's failure — but at what cost, especially in the long term, even to the victors?

The use of power over and against others is thus an inescapable consequence of zero-sum assumptions, as the "arrow" of power always tends to favor selfishness and private accumulation over sharing and social distribution in times of conflict and crisis. Yet in *order* to amass power, it first must be given, ceded, conned, or taken from others. This makes lying, demagogic, and fascistic behaviors, with their aggressive, bullying attitudes toward enemies, competitors, and "outsiders," essential elements in the "primitive accumulation" of power.

The foreseeable side effects of these behaviors and attitudes include ego inflation, loss of perspective, addictive behaviors, grandiosity, megalomania, corruption, sexual harassment, contempt, conspiratorial fantasies, and paranoia. Indeed, in 1964, Richard Hofstadter wrote an influential article on "The Paranoid Style in American Politics," in which he described how paranoia begins by describing a conspiracy to undermine and destroy our very way of life, then proceeds to emulate it:

> The paranoid spokesman sees the fate of conspiracy in apocalyptic terms — he traffics in the birth and death of whole worlds, whole political orders, whole systems of human values. He is always manning the barricades of civilization. He constantly lives at a turning point. Like religious millennialists he expresses the anxiety of those who are living through the last days and he is sometimes disposed to set a date for the apocalypse.

The basis for paranoia and conspiracy theories, Hofstadter argued, can be found in political polarization, perceived isolation, and loss of power:

> Perhaps the central situation conducive to the diffusion of the paranoid tendency [in politics] is a confrontation of opposed interests which are (or are felt to be) totally irreconcilable, and thus by nature not susceptible to the normal political processes of bargain and compromise. The situation becomes worse when the representatives of a particular social interest — perhaps because of the very unrealistic and unrealizable nature of its demands — are shut out of the political process. Having no access to political bargaining or the making of decisions, they find their original conception that the world of power is sinister and malicious fully confirmed. They see only the consequences of power — and this through distorting lenses ...

In these ways, powerful tri-partite alliances are occasionally formed between small coteries of wealthy elites who believe they will lose status, wealth, and power through the ordinary operations of democracy; large groups of angry, frightened voters who feel excluded, shut-out, or bypassed by rights-based majority rule electoral outcomes; and "natural" demagogues and tyrants who use imagined conspiracies, bullying, lies, threats, and appeals to violence to unite them, turning those at the bottom of society into private armies.

In Germany in the 1920s, for example, the first Nazi recruits were those who felt they had been left behind, cast aside, mistreated, and marginalized; those who had fought in World War I and been shamed by defeat; those whose skills were no longer needed or valued; those who were unable to adapt or belong; those who felt lost and powerless, ashamed, and enraged, and readily joined the Brown Shirts and SS.

What Makes Lying, Demagoguery, and Fascism Appealing?

Hannah Arendt described fascism as a temporary alliance between an elite and a mob, yet it is one that crucially relies on demagogues to transform the fear of loss by both into a battle *against* inclusion, truth, and democracy.

In an interesting study of the "The Authentic Appeal of the Lying Demagogue," several researchers, including Oliver Hahl, Minjae Kim, and Ezra W. Zuckerman Sivan, found that demagogues who clearly and deliberately lie are nonetheless seen as positive and regarded as "authentically appealing" by a large number of voters, especially when "one side of a social divide regards the political system as flawed or illegitimate," and the demagogue is seen as an open and flagrant violator of established norms" who is willing to attack the present system, even in violation of "accepted norms of truth-telling" and political decency.

The difficulty with most non- and anti-demagogic responses is that they simply assert or argue in favor of the truth, or science, and miss the vital role lying plays in facilitating the rise of demagogues and fascists. Lying is partly intended to encourage irrationality, in preparation for the suppression of empathy and inclusion, and the instigation of violence against enemies both within and without. More importantly, it serves also as an unambiguous test of personal loyalty and blind obedience, as only those who are unquestioningly loyal and obedient will assert a falsehood simply because the Leader said it.

In a fascinating study of "The Mechanisms of Cult Production," Xavier Márquez at Victoria University in Wellington, New Zealand, examined demagogic, cult — like behaviors in multiple times and countries, and found a number of common features, including "semantic inflation," ego flattery, loyalty signaling, emotional amplification, and similar mechanisms that he saw as a consequence of intense, relatively unstructured competition for the favor of a powerful patron.

Márquez described how these features then combine and interact to transform ordinary flattery into full-blown ruler worship, and how patronage relationships provide fertile ground for the emergence of personality cults. He also revealed how these cults are "directly produced" by using the power of the state and private organizations to grant favors to those who magnify the leader's charismatic qualities and exalted status; or who publicly profess blind loyalty, without question or concern for the facts or circumstances, and thereby increase the legitimacy of dictatorial rule.

One easy way for people to signal their loyalty is by also lying, bullying, attacking, demeaning, and using humiliating personal insults, stereotypes, and slurs against political opponents (subconsciously mirroring their own personal humiliation as flatterers and sycophants), brutalizing relationships, and reducing language to the level of childish taunts. The accepted use of political insults, stereotypes, and slurs then creates a cascade of *additional* unwelcome consequences, including:

- Compression and over-simplification of complex truths
- Use of stereotyping and biases that exaggerate and miss what is true or useful in others views, diminishing the capacity for cooperation
- Granting permission to stop listening and empathizing, and start demonizing and ostracizing minorities and dissenters
- Legitimization and normalization of dishonest, cruel, bullying, patriarchal, power-based forms of political discourse

- Suppression of dialogue and reasoned debate and acceptance of personal attacks, slander, and innuendo, if they serve the cause
- Release from responsibility for whatever they may have done or failed to do that made the problem worse
- Increased apathy, cynicism, and distrust of everything collaborative or mediative that might be proposed to resolve differences
- Increased willingness to accept violence against targeted groups
- Loss of relationships, intimacy and the *capacity* for empathy, caring and collaborative problem solving
- Exhaustion from the energy needed to remain in conflict, keep the truth at bay, and live divided lives
- Inability to evolve and adapt in response to changing conditions
- Loss of hope that anything will ever change

From Lying to Demagoguery to Fascism

While demagogues may manipulate the truth, they still pay lip service to it. For fascists, on the other hand, as described by Robert O. Paxton in *The Anatomy of Fascism*, there is a "radical instrumentalization of the truth," in which the sole criteria becomes the usefulness of the statement in achieving one's goal. It then becomes possible to convert even widely accepted truths into their exact opposites. Moreover, as Hannah Arendt explained,

> It was always a too little noted hallmark of fascist propaganda that it was not satisfied with lying but deliberately proposed to transform its lies into reality. Thus, … [the lie that Jews were homeless beggars and parasites would appear true once German Jews were] driven across the border like a pack of beggars. For such a fabrication of a lying reality no one was prepared. The essential characteristic of fascist propaganda was never its lies, for this is something more or less common to propaganda everywhere and of every time. The essential thing was that they exploited the age-old Occidental

prejudice which confuses reality with truth, and made that 'true" which until then could only be stated as a lie.

Thus, a core element in Nazi propaganda promoted the idea that there was a "Jewish-Christian-Bolshevik conspiracy" based on a "destructive belief in the unity of humanity," and a "false idea of the equality of everyone," which sought to prove itself by dividing people into unequal camps and systematically degrading them. In a more recent example, it was widely asserted that the 2020 Presidential election in the U.S. was stolen, precisely in order to justify trying to steal it; or that ballots were tampered with, in order to then be able to tamper with them.

The transition from lying to demagoguery to fascism can be found in miniature in the conversion of simple personal lies into instruments of power, and the conversion of constitutional government into means for its destruction. It can be seen in the appointment of sycophants to positions of influence and power, and implacable opponents to heads of the agencies they fundamentally oppose, i.e., of foxes to guard the chicken coops. It can especially be observed in the loss of independence and professed neutrality of government agencies charged with legal enforcement, which are sometimes the last defense against the overthrow of democracy.

We may ask, for example, regarding the attempted insurrection in the U.S. on January 6, 2021: What would have happened if senior Trump-installed officials at the Justice Department, especially Acting Attorney General Jeffrey Rosen, had been willing to elevate loyalty to Trump over the rule of law and announce that the 2020 election results were invalid? What if Trump had ousted Rosen and replaced him with Jeffrey Clark, acting head of the Civil Division, who was more willing to make provably false assertions of fraud? What if Trump had not been deterred from doing so when faced with threats of mass resignation from other government officials, including military leaders? What would have happened if Proud Boys and others had gained entrance to Congress, arrested Democratic leaders, confiscated Electoral College ballots; or seized the building and called on Trump to take control? What if the majority Republican Supreme Court had refused to intervene? What if Trump had declared martial law? All these were possible, and each would have "justified" those bent on remaining in power in using illegal and unconstitutional means to do so.

It is important, however, to distinguish the transition from rights-based electoral democracies, with their "customary" forms of political dishonesty; in the first place from demagoguery, with its hostility to the truth and "legal" means of constricting democracy; and in the second place from fascism, with its openly illegal, violent, and dictatorial practices, and elimination of democracy. Jason Stanley described the first step in this process, in *How Propaganda Works,*

> One kind of propaganda, demagogic speech, both exploits and spreads flawed ideologies. Hence, demagogic speech threatens democratic deliberation. A different kind of propaganda, civic rhetoric, can repair flawed ideologies, potentially restoring the possibility of self-knowledge and democratic deliberation.

By "flawed ideologies," Stanley means untrue beliefs that are designed to justify conditions of inequality by actively preventing people from learning the truth about them. These give rise to "undermining propaganda," which embodies abstract democratic ideals while systematically eroding them. Dialogue and "civic rhetoric," on the other hand, reinforce equality, elicit truthful communications, and strengthen democracy.

From a historical perspective, the great social, economic, and political revolutions of the 18th, 19th, and 20th centuries gave rise to a wide range of flawed ideologies and anti-democratic responses, from "no-nothings" and the Ku Klux Klan to eugenics, lynching, race terrorism, social Darwinism, and a wide range of conservative and reactionary political groups and parties.

The primary objectives of these responses were to maximize economic growth, oppose labor unions, promote business deregulation, divide opponents, roll back environmental restrictions, secure tax cuts for the wealthy, create a business friendly Supreme Court, and shape the electoral process in ways that favored conservatives. All of this was done in order to promote capitalism and oppose socialism, which was seen as a consequence of democracy and the steadily increasing electoral power of labor unions and small farmers. James Madison, in an earlier period, described the underlying reasoning behind placing restrictions on electoral democracy:

> The man who is possessed of wealth, who lolls on his sofa, or rolls in his carriage, cannot judge of the wants or feelings of the day laborer. The government we mean to erect is intended to last for ages. ... unless wisely provided against, what will become of your government? In England, at this day, if elections were open to all classes of people, the property of the landed proprietors would be insecure. An agrarian law would soon take place. If these observations be just, our government ought to secure the permanent interests of the country against innovation. Landholders ought to have a share in the government, to support these invaluable interests, and to balance and check the other. They ought to be so constituted as to protect the minority of the opulent against the majority.

This is an ancient pattern, which in the U.S. included turning Whites against Blacks, Latinos, and Asians to undermine the power of labor unions; uniting men to oppose women's right to vote, work, and make independent decisions; and stoking the biases and prejudices of various groups in order to turn them against others, thereby dividing the potential majority their unity might create into separate, inimical, competing minorities.

Over decades, the Supreme Court contributed to the systematic undermining of electoral democracy, by deciding, for example, that campaign contributions by wealthy donors cannot be regulated because they are a form of free speech protected by the First Amendment; or allowing states to adopt gross forms of Gerrymandering to marginalize minority representation; or effectively nullifying the Voting Rights Act and permitting the disenfranchisement of likely Democratic voters, and similar decisions.

In spite of these efforts, rights-based forms of electoral democracy have continued to expand and evolve, yet are facing very real threats that could quite easily come to pass in the near future — the threat, for example, of a shift from "mere" lying and demagoguery to fascism, the overthrow of democracy, and sabotage of the rule of law. How, exactly, does this shift happen? Here, based on historical experience, are some of the initial steps:

- Reduce complex issues to simplistic, adversarial solutions
- Engage in provocative, sensational acts that focus attention on the leader, who will then be feared and unquestioningly obeyed
- Use language that horrifies, shocks, fascinates, distorts, obscures, and draws public attention from the sleight of hand, bait-and-switch, shell game that accrues power through theatre
- Make openly false statements that make it easy to tell who is loyal and who is not
- Instead of responding to accusations of falsehood, move on to fresh lies in a never-ending cycle
- Transform shame into pride, patriotism into nationalism, religion into dogma, race into superiority, and gender into rigid roles and regimentation
- Insult, shame, and humiliate women who are leaders of the opposition
- Encourage acts of violence, directed first against the left, then against liberals, and punish those who do not remain silent or are not complicit in their response
- Manipulate efforts to bring about peace or mediate differences, reject dialogue, and lie about intentions in order to gain advantage over and defeat the other side

In Jason Stanley's subsequent book, *How Fascism Works,* the core elements that make up a generic version of fascism are described in detail (see summary and discussion in Chapter 11.) Ultimately, it is clear that fascism, regardless of its distinct national features and varied definitions, can also be distinguished by its hyper-aggressive, dictatorial, zero-sum approach to differences and conflicts:

> The most telling symptom of fascist politics is division. It aims to separate a population into 'us' and 'them'..., appealing to ethnic, religious and racial distinctions, and using this division to shape ideology, and, ultimately, ... [create] a hierarchy of human worth.

Consequently, the goal of fascism is to destroy — not only equality, collaboration, and democracy, but honesty, authenticity, and interest-based processes like dialogue and mediation as well — and not only in society, economics, politics and the environment — but in family and personal life as well. It does so partly by brutalizing, degrading, and polarizing language in ways that silence complex ideas and experiences. As the linguist Victor Klemperer pointed out, after living under house arrest as a Jew in Germany during most of World War II, and chronicling the ways the Nazi's distorted language,

> ... Nazism permeated the flesh and blood of the people through single words, idioms and sentence structures which were imposed on them in a million repetitions and taken on board mechanically and unconsciously. . . language does not simply write and think for me, it also increasingly dictates my feelings and governs my entire spiritual being the more unquestioningly and unconsciously I abandon myself to it. And what happens if the cultivated language is made up of poisonous elements or has been made the bearer of poisons? Words can be like tiny doses of arsenic: they are swallowed unnoticed, appear to have no effect, and then after a little time the toxic reaction sets in after all. ... [Nazism] changes the value of words and the frequency of their occurrence, it makes common property out of what was previously the preserve of an individual or a tiny group, it commandeers for the party that which was

previously common property and in the process steeps words and
groups of words and sentence structures with its poison.

In order to strengthen dialogue, mediation, and democracy in the
midst of highly polarized political conflicts that produce openings in
the direction of lying, demagoguery, and fascism, it is important to
recognize that democracy, in both its personal and political forms, is
a prerequisite for positive, meaningful change, for dialogue and joint
problem solving, and for mediation itself. We therefore want to
consider how we might redesign the way we approach and respond
to political conflicts, starting with the relationship between
democracy and conflicts regarding race and caste, gender and
patriarchy, wealth, and class. (See longer discussion in Chapter 17.)

Conflicts over Race and Caste, Gender and Patriarchy, Wealth and Class

One of the core functions of the state throughout history has been to
reinforce existing social, economic, political, and ecological
hierarchies in order to preserve privileges, superiority, and
domination, and "keep people in their place." In doing so,
governments have not only prevented racial minorities, women, and
lower classes from voting, but used violence and coercion to stifle
and punish efforts to influence political decisions that seek to bring
about a more fair or favorable ranking system.

In these ways, governments have helped harden internal divides,
turning racial diversity into castes, gender differences into
patriarchies, wealth inequities into classes, etc.. A fundamental
element in the distinction between various forms of government lies
in the degree of openness they offer to alter, adjust, or transform the
ways social status, economic wealth, political power, and
advantageous ecological conditions are earned and distributed.

The essential purpose of dictatorship is therefore to crush as
thoroughly as possible even the *idea* that the current ranking system
can change, whereas democracies open the door, not only to gradual,
reformist, superficial, and evolutionary changes; but to rapid,

radical, systemic, and revolutionary ones. Fascist dictatorships go one step further, and use violence to eliminate the threat of change, impose strict hierarchies to enforce domination and unquestioning obedience, and silence or eliminate anyone who disagrees.

Violence, of course, is a tool, and a natural product of power-based methods of dispute resolution; just as legal coercion is a tool, and a natural product of rights-based methods of dispute resolution. Similarly, democracy, dialogue, consensus building, collaborative negotiation, mediation, restorative justice, and similar techniques, are the principal tools and natural products of interest-based methods of dispute resolution.

We can then see that inequality and domination are essential features of power- and rights-based forms of dispute resolution. Thus, in any society or economy that is based on slavery, or other forms of domination, the state is both designed and compelled to use its primary control over the means of violence and coercion to play one of three possible roles, each representing a phase in its evolution and ability to prevent and resolve chronic conflicts:

1. It can enforce slavery or domination, represent only slave owners or dominators, become a power-base instrument of support for those who seek to enslave or dominate others, and use *autocratic*, adversarial, and violent methods to suppress those who seek change and an end to minority rule.
2. It can seek some form of evolving compromise that allows slavery or domination to continue while recognizing limited rights among slaves or the dominated, claim to be a "neutral" arbitrator between the two sides, and use coercive, bureaucratic, *procedurally* democratic, legalistic methods to defuse conflicts.
3. It can work to abolish slavery and domination, elevate slaves and those who were dominated to full equality, become an instrument of support for those opposed to slavery and domination, and use interest-based *substantively* democratic, collaborative methods to encourage diversity, dissent, and

dialogue, and assist the state in evolving to higher forms of democracy that only become possible once slavery and domination have disappeared.

It is obvious that slavery cannot continue where slaves are given the right to vote. The same is true in the long run for caste, patriarchy, class, and all forms of privilege and domination. As a result, it is essential for minority elites to limit the ability of the majorities they dominate to use the electoral process to abolish domination; or improve their relative status, wealth, and power; or transform elected government in ways that prevent it from being used as a weapon against them.

Thus, democracy itself, when taken seriously and enforced, becomes an implicit and increasing obstacle to the "freedom" to own slaves, suppress women, discriminate against other races, dominate others, and maintain grossly unequal status, inequitable wealth, autocratic power, and ecological advantage over others – especially in periods of conflict and crisis, when the state has to choose whose lives to save, and how taxes will be imposed and spent.

To put it somewhat differently: genuine, interest-based, substantive, participatory, direct, and collaborative forms of democracy are by their nature *levelers*; forces for equality, equity, democracy, and fairness; and they are places of potential transition to non-adversarial, non-zero sum social, economic, political, and ecological relationships and processes. From being a protector of elites and a defender of domination, the state may then increasingly become a mediator, facilitator, and systems designer, whose role is to *prevent* chronic conflicts and crises, and to resolve them through consensus, collaboration, dialogue, and interest-based dispute resolution methods when they do occur.

The State as Mediator

One of the core functions of the state throughout history has been to maintain civic order; stabilize social, economic, political, and ecological relationships; and resolve conflicts; and thereby insulate the status quo against transformational systemic change. It has done so largely by means of power, which is ultimately based on violence; but also by means of rights, which is based on legal coercion and bureaucratic control; and more recently, on the basis of interests, which is based on dialogue, collaborative negotiation, and consensus.

Once we regard the state as a mediator, we can begin to consider how effective it is in settling, resolving, transforming, and preventing chronic social, economic, political, and ecological conflicts; and how it might do so more successfully in the future. We can also recognize that the state may have significant conflicts of interest, and while describing itself as "neutral," may in reality rely heavily on wealthy power brokers in deciding which issues and individuals to support and which to oppose, thereby undermining its ability to resolve conflicts.

Yet were the state to play a significant, genuinely unbiased, mediative role in resolving social, economic, political, and ecological conflicts; were it to adopt an inclusive, collaborative, consensus building, win/win approach to addressing them, it would be able to significantly reduce polarization, discourage violence, hatred, demagoguery, and lying; strengthen substantive democracy; and help dissipate the underlying antagonisms that lead to lying, demagoguery, and fascism.

A key component in its ability to do so will be its adoption and implementation of a number of core values and principles that form the basis for dialogue, collaborative negotiation, consensus building, mediation, and other forms of dispute resolution, and apply them to social, economic, political, and ecological conflicts. In my view, these values and principles include the following:

1. All interested parties are included and invited to participate fully in discussing, designing, and implementing content, processes and relationships
2. Decisions are made by consensus wherever possible, and nothing is considered final until everyone is in agreement

3. Diversity and honest differences are viewed as sources of dialogue, leading to better ideas, healthier relationships, and greater unity

4. Biases, stereotypes, prejudices, assumptions of innate superiority, and ideas of intrinsic correctness are considered divisive and discounted as one-sided descriptions of more complex, multi-sided, paradoxical realities

5. Openness, authenticity, appreciation, and empathy are regarded as better foundations for communication and decision-making than secrecy, rhetoric, insult, and demonization

6. Dialogue and open-ended questions are deemed more useful than debate and cross-examination

7. Force, violence, coercion, aggression, humiliation, and domination are rejected, both as methods and as outcomes

8. Cooperation and collaboration are ranked as primary, while competition and aggression are considered secondary

9. Everyone's interests are accepted as legitimate, acknowledged, and satisfied wherever possible, consistent with others' interests

10. Processes and relationships are considered at least as important as content, if not more so

11. Attention is paid to emotions, subjectivity, and feelings, as well as to logic, objectivity, and facts

12. Everyone is regarded as responsible for participating in improving content, processes, and relationships, and searching for synergies and transformations

13. People are invited into heartfelt communications and deeper awareness, and encouraged to reach resolution, forgiveness, and reconciliation

14. Chronic conflicts are traced to their systemic sources, where they can be prevented and redesigned to discourage repetition

15. Victory is regarded as obtainable by everyone, and redirected toward collaborating to solve common problems, leaving no one feeling defeated

Simply seeking agreement and starting to implement these values and principles will already begin to shift relationships and processes in a more democratic direction, and reduce the likelihood that lying, demagoguery, and fascism will succeed. Unfortunately, fully ending resort to these tactics will not prove so simple, and more will be needed to prevent some future fascist movement from undermining and destroying democracy than simple opposition.

At the center of this problem is a fundamental shift in understanding how conflict resolution works from an emphasis on the mediator as a "neutral," to the mediator as unbiased--or as I prefer, "omni-partial," and thus on both sides at the same time. This does not mean agreeing with everyone factually but focusing on surfacing the underlying non-zero sum interests that make the facts seem compelling.

Rights-based electoral processes and political conflicts encourage people to reduce complex difficulties that may have multiple correct answers to simplistic, digital, either/or, yes or no propositions. Indeed, one of the reasons interest-based methods like mediation and dialogue are not more prevalent, in spite of their obvious benefits, is because they re-introduce complexity, subtlety, and nuance into otherwise simplistic adversarial exchanges, and seek to tell the truth about what is happening without slipping into hostile biases and judgments.

As mediators, we need to check our biases, and subject our beliefs and language to the same level of scrutiny we apply to the beliefs and languages of others. We need to support rational, scientific, and at the same time emotionally intelligent responses to irrational, mythic, and conspiratorial worldviews, and promote open dialogues between people with dramatically opposing views.

In political conflicts particularly, we need to avoid being judgmental and exclusionary, while not concealing or cancelling our own views, or giving in on issues that matter. As mediators, we can either help to clarify the reality of inequality, inequity, autocracy, and domination, or we can obscure them and miss opportunities — not simply to settle, but to resolve, transform, transcend, and prevent conflicts from reoccurring. In order to do so, we need to treat the political statements of both sides as mediators often treat ordinary conflict stories – i.e., as less concerned with factual than with *emotional* accuracy, and as confessions or requests that have been disguised as accusations and insults.

The same can be done with other divisive political issues. We need not allow our desire to connect and be empathetic with both sides to lead us into condoning what we know to be harmful and false. It is possible to demonstrate that we care about people, not by agreeing with the "facts" they assert, but by defining the problem as an "it," rather than a "you;" asking questions that deepen their appreciation of the issues that lie hidden beneath the problem, and similar methods. Guy Burgess of the Beyond Intractability project, for example, proposes the following:

- Reframe zero-sum, us-vs-them interactions in positive-sum, we-are-all-in-this-together ways,
- Show people how to identify and pursue mutually beneficial ways of resolving us-vs-them conflicts,
- Use truth and reconciliation-type processes to move beyond the "unrightable wrongs" of the past,
- Reverse the escalation spiral's amplification of relatively minor disputes in ways that can cross the threshold into mutual hate and violence,
- Correct communication problems that lead people to develop inaccurate and overly threatening images of the "other,"
- Limit factual disagreements through joint data collection and analysis, providing facts that are trustworthy, trusted, and correctly understood,
- Use these trustworthy facts as a basis for collaborative problem-solving efforts that develop mutually beneficial solutions to joint problems.

Laura Nader has criticized mediation as "trading justice for harmony." In my view, that is not, never has been, and never should be the right exchange. Instead, we need to acknowledge the interdependence of justice and peace or harmony, and recognize that, in any relationship, the absence of one will soon result in the absence of the other.

One of the enduring, heartrending sources of human tragedy arises from the assumption that history will continue evolving in the direction it is currently heading. Yet history has multiple sources, with innumerable, complex, contradictory inputs that make it, like the weather, highly sensitive to initial conditions. How many people accurately predicted the 1930's depression while living in the roaring 20's, or the '40s from the 30's, the 50's from the 40's, the 60's from the 50's, etc.? And were not those who did, like the legendary Cassandra in Troy and Mycenae, deadly accurate, but disbelieved by all?

How, then, do we discern an accurate future direction in the midst of our own conflicts and crises? Which of the contradictory undercurrents is likely to become ascendant, for how long, and why? The answer, I believe, depends largely on us, and on our determination to discover and develop successful, interest-based ways of resolving our most pressing social, economic, political, and ecological conflicts. We are one species, one life, one planet, and we urgently need to evolve beyond the adversarial, violent, domineering ways we have treated one another.

20

MEDIATION AND THE LANGUAGE AND CULTURE OF POLITICS

In our age there is no such thing as "keeping out of politics." All issues are political issues, and politics itself is a mass of lies, evasions, folly, hatred, and schizophrenia. When the general atmosphere is bad, language must suffer.

— GEORGE ORWELL

[I]f we use the wrong language, we cannot describe what we are seeing. If we use the language developed for describing fish, we cannot very well describe an elephant: words like "gills," "'scales," and "fins" will not get us very far.

— MASHA GESSEN

[P]eople care less for our beautiful and complex language than they do for the great, crude questions of what is correct and what incorrect. We have ceased to be the poetry lovers we once were, the aficionados of ambiguity and the devotees of doubt, and we have become barroom moralists. Does the thumb point upward? Does it turn down? ... We are all now gladiators in the Coliseum of the Thumb.

— SALMAN RUSHDIE

One of the principal difficulties with political conflicts is that, in addition to disagreements over ideas, facts, proposals, beliefs, and values, there are significant differences in the languages we use to describe ourselves, our opponents, and the issues that divide us; as well as in the disparate cultural norms, expectations, myths, assumptions, and ways we attribute meaning to political ideas and assertions.

These differences in language and culture can be quite apparent, simple, and correctable. It is clear, for example, as journalist Katti Gray writes:

> To change public policy, we also have to change people's thinking, and to change their thinking, we have to change the language they use. . . . When you say 'convict,' a negative image invariably springs into people's minds. If you use only such fraught terms as 'criminal' or 'felon' or 'offender' or 'inmate,' you are suggesting that these are not human beings capable of being redeemed. Words matter ... By changing the language, you change the conversation.

In addition to these relatively clear examples, there are deeper difficulties with the language and culture of politics that are far subtler, more complex, and challenging to address. We can, for example, readily identify dozens of distortions in political language that permeate the speeches of candidates and elected leaders, including these (some suggested by others):

- Broad statements that are so abstract and meaningless they cannot be opposed
- Excessive personalization of issues so they can only be addressed individually
- Negative frameworks that reinforce pessimistic images of the world
- Inculcation of a "learned helplessness" that assumes change is impossible
- Angry, adversarial assumptions that undermine trust
- Strangled or suppressed expression of intense emotions
- Glorification of flags, anthems, and abstract symbols
- Romanticization of the past; of virtues, destiny, and ideals
- Narratives and stories of demonization and victimization
- All or nothing assumptions that eliminate common ground
- Attacks directed at critics and independent media
- Repeated references in noble, *basso profundo* tones, to "our country," "the mother / fatherland," or "the people of the United States of America" (or wherever)
- Denials of wrongdoing and cover-ups
- Laying blame for failures on opponents and claiming credit for their successes
- Crass manipulations of maudlin sentimentality, particularly regarding children, struggling families, religious figures, the nation's history, and recently departed political leaders
- Facades of personal outrage and affront about others
- Loud protestations and harsh denunciations of moral transgressions committed by others
- Assertions of uncompromising toughness
- Simplistic, formulaic responses and unyielding principles regarding complex, multilayered, shifting problems
- Demands for punishment of opponents
- Crass use of religious sentiments and divine support for our nation
- Sanctimony and self-righteousness combined with false humility
- Calls for immediate action by others

Yet these very excesses and distortions of political language, through their exaggerated, stultifying rhetoric, suggest the need for deeper dialogue, change, and learning. As Toni Morrison brilliantly wrote regarding the language of war, but with equal applicability to the language of politics:

> No matter the paid parades, the forced applause, the instigated riots, the organized protests (pro or con), self- or state censoring, the propaganda; no matter the huge opportunities for profit and gain; no matter the history of injustice – at bottom it is impossible to escape the suspicion that the more sophisticated the weapons of war, the more antiquated the idea of war. The more transparent the power grab, the holier the justification, the more arrogant the claims, the more barbaric, the more discredited the language of war becomes.

The Language of Politics

Part of the problem is that the aggressive, adversarial languages adopted by power- and rights-based systems not only render them incapable of collaboratively solving problems, but dissuade others from trying to do so. The difficulty is therefore one of *inventing*, basically from scratch, interest-based, collaborative, values-oriented, mediative political languages, cultures, and problem-solving processes that can address global problems more rapidly and collaboratively.

As described in Chapter 7, the language favored by power-based organizations such as the military, police, and monarchical states requires clarity, simplicity, and uniform interpretation in order to encourage unthinking obedience. The communications that emanate from these institutions therefore take the form of declarations, propaganda, pronouncements, and orders, which reinforce hierarchy and command, and imply punishment and contempt for those who disobey.

On the other hand, the language favored by rights-based organizations such as legal institutions, bureaucracies, and formally democratic states, requires narrow distinctions, exceptions, and adjudicated interpretations in order to maintain control by permitting some behaviors and forbidding others. The communications that emanate from these institutions take the form of rules and regulations, policies and procedures, legislative definitions, adversarial arguments, and legal interpretations, which reinforce bureaucracy and control and imply coercion and censure for those who do not fit in.

By contrast, the language favored by interest-based organizations such as teams, civil society, and radically democratic states, requires affirmation of diversity, dissent, and dialogue in order to encourage collaboration and participation. The communications that emanate from these institutions take the form of open-ended questions, open dialogues, value-driven rules, conversations, and consensus decision-making, which reinforce social equality, economic equity, and political democracy.

In fascism, power-based political language assumes a more *intentionally* destructive form, as described in detail by Victor Klemperer in his powerful book, *Language of the Third Reich*, which identified, among others, the following glaring distortions in Nazi political language:

- Legitimizing hatred and rage directed toward racial, religious, sexual, or ethnic groups such as Jews, Blacks, Gypsies, Gays, and others
- Generally debasing and "dumbing down" language to the level that is used by children in order to shame and ostracize others
- Militarizing and brutalizing common speech
- Promoting fear and disgust toward immigrants and foreigners
- Discounting reason and elevating feelings
- Repetitive stereotyping, emotional superlatives, use of romantic adjectives and personal insults
- Using "big lies," implausible denials and doublespeak

- Hijacking or poisoning formerly positive terms such as "social," "collective," "followers," and "faith"
- Transforming formerly negative words into positives, such as "domination," "fanatical," and "obedient"

Joseph Goebbels, chief propagandist for the Nazi Party, described the fascist objective quite clearly:

> If you tell a lie big enough and keep repeating it, people will eventually come to believe it. The lie can be maintained only for such time as the State can shield the people from the political, economic and/or military consequences of the lie. It thus becomes vitally important for the State to use all of its powers to repress dissent, for the truth is the mortal enemy of the lie, and thus by extension, the truth is the greatest enemy of the State.

And Adolph Hitler, in Mein Kampf, went further:

> All propaganda must be so popular and on such an intellectual level, that even the most stupid of those toward whom it is directed will understand it. Therefore, the intellectual level of the propaganda must be lower the larger the number of people who are to be influenced by it.... Through clever and constant application of propaganda, people can be made to see paradise as hell, and also the other way round, to consider the most wretched sort of life as paradise.

One of the foremost differences between "ordinary" political lies and the "big lie" technique described by Goebbels, Hitler, and others, is that fascist governments use language and violence in combination to force people to *live* their lies. Statements that are obviously deceptive, deceitful, duplicitous, and divided become mandatory and routine, and are reframed as honest, straightforward, reliable, and unified, creating what Gregory Bateson called "double binds" that *immediately* make anyone who does not comply easily identifiable, indisputably wrong, and vulnerable to attack.

Everyone is compelled by coercive and violent means to *internalize* and *enact* the lie, vigorously defend it against the truth, and force others to accept its correctness. This permits a form of political control that is near total, and eliminates the need for universal monitoring, as it forces people to surrender all independent thought and ensures their advance support for whatever illegal, unconstitutional, and unjust actions may be employed.

One of the primary tasks of conflict resolvers is therefore to *reframe* power- and rights-based political languages in ways that support a transition to more interest-based, egalitarian, collaborative, and democratic communications. As mediators, we already know many of the elements needed to do this, but have yet to put them together in ways that are politically compelling and capable of overcoming entrenched, insurgent, and authoritarian groups, whose desire for power and domination *invite* adversarial, demagogic, and dishonest forms of political discourse. [For more on language and politics, see discussion in *Conflict Revolution: Designing Preventative Solutions for Social, Economic, and Political Conflicts*, and *Politics, Dialogue, and the Evolution of Democracy*]

Alternative Forms of Advocacy, Rhetoric, and Discourse

The language of politics largely consists of one-sided statements of positions, advocacy of adversarial outcomes, rhetorical arguments for and against, angry denunciations of opponents, partisan declarations of fact and law, closed-ended questions, stereotypes and biases against others, emotional appeals for support, egotistical grandstanding, and efforts to persuade those in the middle to join forces in defeating the opposition.

More than two millennia ago, Aristotle identified three primary forms of advocacy, rhetoric, and persuasion, which are routinely used in adversarial legal and political discourse today. These are:

1. *Logos*: Arguments based on logic or reason, or on evidence such as facts or figures. Yet is it common for lawyers and politicians to play fast-and-loose with logic and with facts

and figures, and for fact checking and corrections to go unnoticed.

2. *Ethos*: Arguments based on character, or ethics, or credibility and expertise. Yet legal and political arguments often place a premium on character assassination, ignore ethical violations, and discount proven credibility and expertise.

3. *Pathos*: Arguments based on emotion or feelings. Yet powerful negative feelings like fear and anger can easily be stirred up by adversarial legal and political processes, and overwhelm rationality.

Through mediation practice, dialogue facilitation, and other interest-based forms of communication, we have discovered that it is possible to reframe and shift these approaches in the direction of collaborative outcomes by using alternative approaches to advocacy, rhetoric, and persuasion, including:

1. *Personal Experience and Empathy*, chiefly through storytelling, dialogue and empathetic listening

2. *Vision and Values*, chiefly through leadership, commitment and modeling

3. *Synergy and Syntheses*, chiefly through conflict resolution and the integration of competing ideas

4. *Beauty and Symmetry*, chiefly through the arts, sciences and mathematics

5. *Love and Caring*, chiefly through kindness, heartfelt interactions, shared intimacy, and reciprocity in relationships

The outcome of these alternative approaches to advocacy, rhetoric, and persuasion is the emergence of languages, cultures, and forms of discourse that are multi-sided, collaborative, and non-binary; that search for shared meanings, ask open-ended questions, acknowledge and learn from opponents, critique biases and stereotypes, encourage honesty and authenticity, and aim for consensus-based outcomes that are acceptable to all.

If we ask, what is *better* than advocacy, rhetoric, and persuasion, the answer is a *dialogue,* sparked by a finely honed question, that *might* lead to self-discoveries, profound realizations, fresh insights, heightened awareness, new ways of thinking, creative forms of problem solving, increased ownership, discovery of complex truths, transformation and transcendence of the conflict, improved capacity for communication and collaboration, more trusting and satisfying relationships, learning and wisdom, deeper humility, increased skills, enhanced civility, and a search for personal, relational, and systemic improvement.

Two Meanings of Civility

It is also essential for us to find ways of responding imaginatively to the *superficially* civil, legalistic, and bureaucratic, rights-based languages that are commonly used by conflict-averse organizations and institutions to stall, sideline, dishearten, undermine, and punish efforts to bring about systemic change. We need to invent and discover words and phrases that will resonate with voters who seem to oscillate between being apathetic and avoidant, scared and distrustful, proud, and aggressive, or enraged and punishing, all of which are elicited, strengthened, and sustained by political language.

These adversarial power- and rights-based languages and polarized cultures of politics are sometimes used simply as a cover for playing it safe, or to hide from the consequences of what needs to be done. Yet our customary practice as mediators is to invite people, implicitly and explicitly, to shift their languages and cultures from an orientation to adversarial power-based battles; or rights-based civility, conformity, and passive compliance; to interest-based exploration, dissent, and ownership.

It is important, however, to clarify what we mean by "civility," as at least two meanings are possible. First, it can suggest conflict suppression and a retreat to superficial politeness that marginalizes intense emotions and prioritizes accommodation and compromise. Second, it can denote conflict *engagement* and a shift to respectful, open, honest conversations about values, beliefs, and feelings that are affirming, empathetic, inclusive, diverse, and collaborative.

Each of these definitions leads to vastly different languages, cultures, and outcomes, both in politics and in personal relationships. At the core of the first is often a fear of confrontation and the negative emotions that flow from adversarial, win/lose power- and rights-based arguments; while the second reveals a deep-seated recognition of the *generative* value of dissent, differences of opinion, and the positive emotions and improved outcomes that emanate from collaborative, win/win, interest-based processes and relationships.

To encourage the use of these interest-based processes and relationships, it is important to identify a few core lessons from past responses to political conflicts. First, it is *not* helpful for mediators to use civility to silence or minimize the passion and commitment people feel for what they believe in or want for the world. Second, it *is* helpful for mediators to use civility to try and redirect peoples' passions and commitments from attacking their opponents to understanding what is beneath the surface of their emotions, beliefs, and desires, and search together for principles on which they can agree. Third, it is also helpful to use civility to remind ourselves that we are members of the same family, we belong to the same species, and all live on the same planet, and sooner or later, we will *have* to find ways of solving problems together if we are to survive. Fourth, the ability to discuss, negotiate, and resolve differences civilly is *foundational*, not only to mediated problem solving but to collaboration and democracy. Fifth, changing the *ways* we speak to each other about our differences can vastly improve all our communications, dialogues, negotiations, problem solving efforts, and mediations, and help overcome impasse and intractability. Sixth, conventional political language promotes one-sided, partisan support for a single person's or party's ideas, assertions, and proposals, and we need to strengthen civil ways of affirming everyone's right to have the ideas they believe in discussed, considered, tested, and then either adopted, amended, synthesized, or discarded.

Without these core ideas, it is easy to lose touch with empathy and slip into uncivil, adversarial political arguments, or to stand civilly and passively by as angry, hostile groups use their freedom of speech uncivilly, *precisely* in order to destroy it for others — as the Nazi's consciously did in Germany in the 1920s and 30's. Unfortunately, as history amply demonstrates, failing to defend our opponents' right to speak legitimizes them in later denying it to us and makes the abrogation and annulment of democracy far more likely. Worse, it cheats everyone out of the opportunity to turn conflict avoidance and authoritarian monologues into conflict engagement and democratic dialogues, reinforcing the subtle fascistic attitudes that destroy civility in order to promote violence and silence their opposition, even at the subtle level of processes and relationships.

In the end, whatever *connects* us empathetically and collaboratively across our differences will predictably result in reducing our capacity for fear and hatred, which are the deeper truths of our incivility and hostility toward others. Nietzsche interestingly wrote that the best way to enrage people is to force them to change their minds about you. This seems especially true in politics and is a principal difficulty in our work as mediators, as we can see in conflicts over civility and respect, bias and prejudice, and exclusive, hostile, argumentative cultures of political correctness.

Cultures of Political Correctness

When politics is limited to elections, and democracy is confined to voting yes or no, for or against, this party or that, my candidate or yours, political language and culture *automatically* become binary, digital, flat, crude, and adversarial, reducing our ability to solve complex, subtle, multi-dimensional problems, and demoting them to clashes over cursory, overly simplistic, falsely polarized, one-dimensional proposals.

These stunted, power- and rights-base languages and cultures block genuine engagement, dialogue, and popular decision-making, and increasingly turn democracy into an empty shell that can easily be manipulated by elites, autocrats, and corrupt politicians. Each side assumes there is a single, unitary, exclusive, invariant truth that consists solely in what they alone are saying; or even more trivially, in the dogmatic, propagandistic, formulaic *ways* they say it. In the process, complex meanings are simplified, distorted, and disguised, taking the form of repeated, coded phrases and covert "dog whistles," representing veiled political goals that are undisclosed, undiscussed, and undefined, yet inferred and understood.

While these distorted political languages and cultures of "political correctness," are commonly attributed to the left, they are actually found in all parties, groups, and factions of the left, right, and middle. Each insists on using words and phrases that reinforce their particular values and beliefs without explicitly saying so, and in these ways create easy sources of group identity, mass conformity, social cohesion, ostracism, and personal anonymity.

These political languages can be critiqued as efforts to create a single objective standard for everyone in deciding which political ideas and acts are ethically or factually correct and which are not; or alternately, as an unstated, yet logically necessary assumption that political ideas in general are pluralistic, unscientific, and therefore *incapable* of being proved either ethical or unethical, true or false, correct or incorrect, based on objective evidence that others are likely to find convincing.

Yet accusations of political correctness can also be seen as *requests* for more respectful relationships; invitations into open dialogue and joint problem solving; unconscious efforts to move beyond power-based hostile and demeaning biases and stereotypes; or criticisms of historically dated rights-based political orthodoxies, superficialities, and subliminal slurs.

Regardless of the underlying reasons for these accusations, logically there are only six possible outcomes of any effort to determine which of two competing political propositions is correct:

1. The first is correct and the second is incorrect
2. The second is correct and the first is incorrect

3. Both are incorrect
4. Both are correct
5. Neither is correct or incorrect
6. Both are correct and incorrect in different ways

The first two options, which underlie most accusations of political correctness, commonly result in efforts to counter or suppress the "incorrect" act, statement, or idea, sometimes by force, and impose a win/lose outcome that rejects the losing proposition entirely, castigates and punishes those who spoke or acted incorrectly, and generally ends the conversation without dialogue, learning, synergy, or improvement.

The third and fifth options also end the conversation prematurely, unless we go deeper and critique the underlying belief that it is possible to determine, in a scientific way, whether a given political statement is actually correct or incorrect. More often, these assumptions take a simplistic, cynical, middle-of-the-road position favored by bureaucrats, journalists, political pundits, and frightened voters, and dismiss the "extreme" views on both sides, often out of cowardice rather than conviction, and a fear of being attacked or ostracized for taking an unpopular position.

The fourth option moves us a little nearer to the core problem of trying to establish the truth of political assertions, which are not, as Isaiah Berlin argued, mathematical or scientific *in nature*; that is, they are generally non-quantifiable, non-provable, and non-falsifiable. This option has the defect that it may also end the conversation at the precise moment when it might become useful – that is, at what mediators recognize as the source, center, or crux of the conflict, where it is most likely to lead to genuine communication, insight, learning, and growth.

I find the sixth option more useful because it captures the complexity, subtlety, hidden dimensionality, and paradoxical nature of most political conflicts, whose correctness or "truth," frequently takes the form of a "complementarity," a term coined and defined by

Nobel Prize winning physicist Neils Bohr as, "a great truth whose opposite is also a great truth."

In other words, what is fundamentally *correct* about all deeply held political beliefs and assertions is that they represent one out of many possible interpretations of the meaning of a set of subjective experiences; or particular ideas and options for the future that might be modified and retooled to include others. These are accompanied by a latent defect in the adversarial *form* of their presentation, which can give rise to opposition for reasons that are not always entirely conscious, clear, or constructive.

What is fundamentally *incorrect* about all deeply held political assertions is that they do not acknowledge or include the opposite "complementary" truths advanced by others, who are stereotyped as misguided and regarded as adversaries. As a result, they are not yet "whole" truths, but incomplete, immature, "larval" forms that have yet to experience the syntheses and transformations that are uniquely triggered by communication, dialogue, joint problem solving, collaboration, negotiation, and mediation.

John Stuart Mill wrote, several centuries ago, that, "It is not the violent conflict between parts of the truth, but the quiet suppression of half of it that is the formidable evil." And the half we are most eager to suppress, often out of a desire for certainty and simplicity, or a deeply held belief in some ethical or moral principle, is the half that transforms the truth we insist on into a more nuanced, subtle, complex, enigmatic, evolved, and *beautiful* form that runs deeper and lasts longer than the half we are holding on to so dearly; the one we dress up and distort until it becomes a caricature and turns false, even as it is spoken.

What, then, are the "politically correct" assertions people complain about so bitterly? Often they are simply subjective truths, i.e., painful life experiences, passionately held ideas, or intense unacknowledged emotions, together with a lack of skill in communicating them successfully to others, whose *equally* valid experiences, ideas, and emotions draw them in different directions. Yet it is possible to design conversations that result in listening, learning, and encourage people to discover higher orders of truth that *only* emerge when they creatively combine their opposing truths.

This does not mean that genuine factual, mathematical, or scientific truths do not exist; or that what other people think and feel is not true for them; or that there is no truth other than experience and opinion; or that political beliefs are superior to reality; or that compromise always leads to higher truths. On the contrary, among the universally accepted criteria for factual, mathematical, and scientific truths is the idea that they should lead to unique predictions that can be tested, or as Karl Popper asserted, falsified. Once these higher levels of truth have been established, no denial, no matter how rigorously imposed, can maintain it forever.

Moreover, none of these truths is made any truer by combining opposing propositions in some bland, cursory, mediocre compromise that denies their opposition; or by reducing them to conventional banalities, clichés, and platitudes; or by adulterating whatever accuracy they may once have possessed; or by reducing them to sterile, neutered forms that eliminate conflicts by stripping them of all their deeper meanings and consequences.

Higher forms of combination take place when conflicts are transformed in ways that invite them to assume non-zero-sum forms that capture their complexity; strip them of their destructive potential; focus their energy on diverse, collaborative, interest-based approaches to problem-solving; and encourage critical examination, learning, and improvement.

As a consequence, there are *two* principle methods for combining opposites: first, in a simplistic way through compromise, as by adding cold water to hot water and producing lukewarm water; or second, in a more complex way through synthesis, as by adding water, flour, yeast, and heat and creating bread. It is the second that allows us to *resolve* our conflicts, and becomes possible through dialogue, collaborative negotiation, mediation, and similar techniques. What allows us to transition from lukewarm solutions to those that create bread is our ability to discover or design *questions* that invite adversaries to shift from power- to rights- to interest-based approaches to conflict resolution.

In *all* disputes, including those that are social, economic, political, and environmental, it is possible for mediators to identify a set of "pivot points" that take the form of "dangerous" questions around which conflicts can turn, and shift from being intractable to being resolvable. For example, it is possible to transform adversarial, zero-sum political conversations over contested facts or beliefs by asking questions that focus on shared values, common interests, and subjective experiences; or on the problem as an "it" rather than as a "you;" or by reframing divisive, polarizing, exclusively correct languages. Our inability to make these shifts can cause mediations to fail, keep us at impasse, divert attention to blaming others; and block us from addressing chronic conflicts at their systemic sources.

Why Political Mediations Sometimes Fail

To fully understand any method, process, or technique and implement it effectively, we need to probe its limits and push it to the point where it begins to break down, allowing us to discover in its decomposition something of its true nature. [For more on this process and the limits of mediation, see Chapter 21.]

It is important to begin by admitting that mediation is not a cure-all, or snake oil that can lubricate all social ills. While conflict resolution methods are nearly always beneficial, even when they don't result in agreements, are there political times when they are not? Under what circumstances might conflict actually be *preferable* to settlement, compromise, or partial, truncated solutions?

What, for instance, of the mediation in Munich between Hitler and Mussolini representing Germany and Italy, versus Chamberlain and Daladier for England and France? Was it appropriate for Mussolini to act as the mediator? Was trading the defense of Czechoslovakia for predictably false promises of peace a successful compromise? Who was, and was not at the table when that decision was made, and what difference would their inclusion in the mediation have made? What would a *genuine* mediation or full resolution of that conflict have looked like? Who would have had to have been present? Could a different approach have led to a different result?

What about the many efforts to mediate the growing conflicts that took place over slavery before the U.S. Civil War, all of which offered guarantees for the continued legality of slavery? What about the conflicts that took place over apartheid in South Africa prior to the release of Nelson Mandela, or over colonialism in India before independence? Would it have been possible in those circumstances to reach full and genuine resolutions through ordinary mediation and dialogue? How might we mediate serious losses of status, wealth, power, and environmental advantage? What should the role of mediation be in highly polarized political conflicts that are gravitating towards war? How do we know whether, or when, instead of producing a resolution, mediation might actually bring about a loss of hope or trust, and a continuation of the conflict?

Or, on a smaller and more personal scale, what would mediation *before* the event consist of, for example, between a murderer and his or her innocent intended victim? What of the rape victim, the slum tenant who resides with rats, or the parents of a molested child? Are "win-win" approaches always possible, and what do we do if they aren't? When does compromise become unacceptable and conflict preferable? When does neutrality mean siding with the powerful against the powerless?

In my experience as a participant in the political movements of the 1960's, including the civil rights movement in the South and the North, there were many occasions when confrontation felt necessary and useful, for example, in drawing attention to injustice, or bringing people to the negotiating table, or offering dignity and a voice to people who would otherwise have been silenced and ignored. All these, in hindsight, can be seen as essential steps in securing deeper and more lasting resolutions by using conflict as a means of calling attention — not only to important problems, but their underlying chronic, systemic sources.

Through these examples, we can recognize that, not only for us as individuals; and for marriages, families, workplaces, and interpersonal relationships; but also for organizations, cultures, societies, economies, polities, and environments, there are times when conflicts *need* to be expressed in order to expose their chronic underlying sources, and thereby make deeper, genuine, and *complete* resolutions possible.

This is not to suggest that destructive conflicts ought to continue indefinitely without making strenuous efforts at resolution; or that peacemaking is not a fundamental goal; but that there are limits on the desirability of compromising and settling conflicts *prematurely*, without achieving just outcomes; or surfacing their hidden secrets; or revealing the preventative possibility of ending their chronic, systemic repetition; and, that it may sometimes be necessary even to *increase* the level of conflict in order to discover how to resolve it more completely and lastingly.

We can therefore broaden our definition of the role of conflict resolvers to include not merely stopping or settling conflicts, but helping people discover the language they need to constructively *express* them, open them up, expose their hidden natures, encourage principled opposition to their chronic sources, design systemic improvements, and end their long-term destructiveness. In the process, we will discover that there are ways of disagreeing and fighting more *positively* and productively, intelligently and competently, collaboratively and synergistically — not over relatively superficial and mundane issues; but their hidden sources, enduring elements, and *essential* natures, and learn how to transform, transmute, transcend, and prevent them.

Doing so will require us to shift the entire *nature* of political discourse, in part by incorporating principles of emotional intelligence, dialogue facilitation, consensus building, mediation, and the sensitivity and depth of poetry into the coarse and profane language of politics. Poet Reginald Dwayne Betts writes,

I want to say that language is politics, but that seems not to be true. Or it seems to suggest that everything is politics and if everything is politics, then nothing is politics. So maybe the way I understand the two is this: for me, the language of poetry is what allows me to recognize something about politics I hadn't before.

If poetics and politics represent unique truths, the creation of a language that combines them could produce profound results. Henry David Thoreau was said to have kept two books, one for facts and one for poems, and to have sought some day to merge them, so that every poem would be a fact, and every fact would be a poem. I cannot imagine a better future for the language of politics.

21

THE LIMITS OF MEDIATION

Every man takes the limits of his own field of vision for the limits of the world.

— ARTHUR SCHOPENHAUER

To be aware of limitations is already to be beyond them.

— GEORG WILHELM FRIEDRICH HEGEL

The only way of discovering the limits of the possible is to venture a little way past them into the impossible.

— ARTHUR C. CLARKE

I t is difficult to understand anything fully until we recognize its limits — the places where it falls apart, or miraculously comes together — where it begins and ends or transforms into something entirely different. Together, these limits define the frontiers, or *terra incognita*, where critical discoveries can be made, and entirely new and profound understandings can take shape. As I wrote several years ago in *Mediating Dangerously,*

> It is difficult to describe what happens when things fall apart, or how they turn, transform themselves and come together in new ways. Words cannot accurately account for what happens at the edges, the frontiers and boundaries, the dark places where everything we know crumbles and disintegrates, or the bright places at the center where what we didn't know coalesces and becomes something new.

Mediation encompasses both. Conflicts mark the frontiers, the places where we weaken and divide. Yet these same frontiers embody the forces that strengthen us, bring us together, transform us, and dissipate our differences. Conflicts probe our innermost natures, and the outermost limits of our being. They provoke cruelty and compassion, competition and collaboration, revenge and reconciliation. Mediation is the *dangerous* magic that moves us from one to the other.

Perhaps the greatest limit in any endeavor is created by what we *think* we know, which leads us to fail to notice anything different or contradictory, anything that might require a fresh approach or paradigm or understanding. What is worse, we do not know that we do not know. As Psychiatrist R. D. Laing described it,

> The range of what we think and do is limited by what we fail to notice. And because we fail to notice that we fail to notice, there is little we can do to change until we notice how failing to notice shapes our thoughts and deeds.

It is therefore important for us to develop an understanding of the limits – not just of mediation as a process, but of the ways we perceive and think about conflicts that defeat our imagination and prevent discovery. Mediation is still in its infancy, and because we are still beginners in this work, we don't actually know what the limits of the process are. However, we can start by identifying some likely, or potential limits, which I prefer to think of as *dualities* that appear disconnected, yet are invisibly linked, and can be approached and considered from different perspectives that illuminate, enhance, and complement each other.

Two of the fundamental limits in every human endeavor are biases and noise. Daniel Kahneman, who won the Nobel Prize in economics, wrote brilliantly about biases in *Thinking Fast and Slow.* Subsequently, in *Noise: A Flaw in Human Judgment,* Kahneman, with Olivier Sibony and Cass R. Sunstein, wrote that to appreciate and correct errors in judgment, it is necessary to understand both bias and noise. Bias, of which there are many varieties, creates errors in judgment, but so does noise, which is rarely discussed or acknowledged.

The authors define noise as "unwanted variability" that we bring to decision-making, including random errors of judgment that can lead to compromised fairness, decision risks, and uncertainty. The difficulty is that conflict is both a fertile source of bias and naturally noisy. They write, with particular relevance for mediators,

> Some noise may be inevitable in practice, a necessary side effect of a system ... that gives each case individualized consideration, that does not treat people like cogs in a machine, and that grants decision makers a sense of agency ... Diversity of opinions is essential for generating ideas and options. Contrarian thinking is essential to innovation.

In mediation, it is possible to reduce the impact of both bias and noise by paradoxically *increasing* the amount of variability, adding alternative ideas and diverse interpretations, and expanding the range of available choices. This suggests a shift from rules to standards, which the authors distinguish as follows:

> Rules are meant to eliminate discretion by those who apply them; standards are meant to grant such discretion. Whenever rules are in place, noise ought to be severely reduced ... [However], whenever a public or private institution tries to control noise through firm rules,

it must always be alert to the possibility that the rules will simply drive discretion underground.

Mediation, in my view, makes it possible to transform the parties' focus from imposing or obeying rules to clarifying, negotiating, and committing to values. We may then regard the limits of mediation as requiring a similar shift from identifying simple, fixed, clear, logical, one-dimensional situations in which we cannot succeed to posing a set of complex, fluid, imprecise, poetic, multi-dimensional paradoxes where some limits exist, but in a form can be bypassed or worked through, as regularly happens, for example, in quantum tunneling.

As an inspiration for the limits described below, Gandhi created an interesting list of "seven social sins." These included: wealth without work, pleasure without conscience, knowledge without character, commerce without morality, science without humanity, religion without sacrifice, and politics without principle.

If we imagine a similar list for mediation, each limit may then be described as an interconnected set of concerns, without finally deciding whether any particular issue is mediate-able or not. Instead, each limit ought to allow us to reframe the problem, look at our experiences with fresh eyes, be willing to try something completely new, make repeated efforts that may appear unlikely to succeed, and learn afresh what is mediate-able and what is not in each circumstance, based on subtle, complex, continually shifting conditions.

Here, then, is my top ten list of the likely limits of mediation, with a brief explanation of each that identifies the difficulty without eliminating the possibility that innovate efforts may succeed in resolving it.

1. *Power without purpose.* Power is an obstacle in mediation because it is nearly always unequally distributed and arranged as a "zero-sum game," or "win/lose" process. If resort to power has a purpose, it may be possible to achieve that purpose by satisfying the parties' interests and thereby

reduce their perceived need to resort to power. Yet where power is used without any goal or purpose at all, as when it is exercised simply for the pleasure of defeating others, satisfying interests will be less likely to prevent people from using it.

2. *Insanity without comprehension.* Everyone in conflict is a little bit crazy, or seems so to their opponent, so describing the other person as insane doesn't mean we are off the hook in trying to mediate, because there is a small piece of insanity that is triggered by every emotional confrontation that can be assuaged by expanding their comprehension – of self, of others, and of the problem. Yet where insanity precludes all comprehension or obstructs the ability to understand what is taking place at all, we may not be able to mediate, and consensus will become elusive.

3. *Dishonesty without motive.* Dishonesty that has an underlying motive or goal can be addressed by seeking to satisfy it, in which case the person will feel less strong a need to be dishonest. An example might be someone who lies about what time it is, or about the weather for no discernable reason. People in conflict lie to each other often, particularly where dishonesty is motivated by survival, or their desire to retain a job, or keep a marriage, or be promoted, or be loved or looked on favorably by others. Yet where there is dishonesty without any motive at all, it is far more difficult to prevent people from using it.

4. *Addiction without awareness.* People can become addicted to many things, including conflict, yet if we are able to increase awareness of their addiction, we may be able to design a process like Alcoholics Anonymous' 12-step program, or some other method that can assist the person or organization in breaking their addiction. Yet if they are addicted and resist becoming aware of how addicted they are, or how addiction works, or how it impacts others, their unawareness and resistance can limit our ability to resolve the conflict.

5. *Greed without gain.* If someone is seeking gain from greed, a

mediator may be able to find a way of getting them what they need or want without needing to become greedy. In this case, their greed is actually *conditional*, contingent, and instrumental rather than absolute, fixed, and fundamental. Yet if they are greedy without any desire for gain, their insatiability can create obstacles to empathy, learning, and collaboration that limit the effectiveness of mediation.

6. *Suffering without empathy.* In the beginning, people who suffer turn inward, often obstructing their ability to feel empathy or compassion for the suffering of others. Suffering can lead to an increase in our capacity to recognize pain in others and experience empathy and compassion for them., which can diminish the length and depth of suffering by transforming it into increased sensitivity. Yet to suffer without any ability to experience empathy or compassion for the suffering of others often blocks listening, understanding, and acknowledgement, and creates limits in mediation.

7. *Revenge without self-interest.* Revenge, in my view, is the willingness to hurt ourselves in order to hurt others. The introduction of any form of self-interest, self-esteem, or self-care can therefore begin to undermine the desire for revenge. But to be so deeply and passionately committed to revenge and the pain of others that we are willing to harm ourselves can make it much more difficult, if not impossible, to mediate successfully.

8. *Trauma without meaning.* When trauma feels meaningless, it is difficult for those who experience it to perceive its deeper lessons and possibilities, leaving them unable to cope with, escape, learn from, or transcend it. If suffering can be seen to have a larger meaning or higher purpose, perhaps in our commitment to making sure that no one else experiences the same injury again, it may be possible to mediate restorative solutions. Yet to suffer trauma without any meaning at all can keep people feeling trapped in suffering and reduce the effectiveness of mediation.

9. *Bias without perception.* Everyone has biases of many different

kinds, ranging from simple cognitive biases to more serious
stereotypes, prejudices, and discriminatory attitudes that
assert superiority based on race, gender, sexual orientation,
caste, class, religion, nationality, age, disability, and similar
criteria. The worst biases occur in those who do not perceive
that they are biased, or are unaware or deny they even exist.
Perception of bias reduces its strength by inviting us to see
others as more complex, unique, and human than our bias
can comprehend. Yet being biased without perception creates
obstacles to mutual understanding that can reduce the ability
to mediate authentic agreements.

10. *Emotion without insight.* People in conflict experience a broad
range of emotions from mild to intense, including anger and
fear, sadness and grief, shame and guilt, and many others.
When we are in the grips of these intense emotions, we can
lose insight into their deeper, underlying sources;
perspective on what they mean to the people who receive
them; and ability to assess what we could do to assuage,
transform, and transcend them. Insight, perspective, and
assessment can help us turn our emotions in toward problem
solving. Yet experiencing intense emotions without any
insight, perspective, or assessment at all can make it difficult
to assist people in *completing* and passing through them.

11. *Domination without dialogue.* The desire to dominate,
manipulate, and control others without allowing dialogue or
dissent, in ways that exclude, silence, or annihilate the
interests and perspectives of others, effectively reduces two
parties to one and eliminates all the insights and synergies
that can emerge when their diversities are brought together.
Yet domination, manipulation, and control without any
willingness to engage in dialogue with those who are being
dominated, manipulated, or controlled undermines the core
values and principles of mediation and creates power
imbalances that make it difficult to solve problems and find
common ground.

12. *Politics without principle.* This limit, first suggested by

Gandhi, acknowledges that politics, like mediation, may require people to compromise and reach agreement with their opponents. Principles guide politics and direct the problem solving process, even for opponents. Yet when we compromise what we believe in and negotiate away our principles, we strip politics of its redeeming potential, lose opportunities to make our lives better, and reduce our righteous, high-sounding rhetoric to opportunistic searches for short-term advantage.

There are many other possible limits in mediation, including those produced by extreme rigidity and dogmatism, excessive vulnerability and emotional fragility, strong needs to control and manipulate others, extreme narcissism and paranoia, a desire to shame and humiliate others, hostile styles of advocacy and negotiation, the incompatibility of languages, avoidant and adversarial cultures of conflict, dogmatism and orthodoxy, etc. Yet for each of these limits, as for all the others, there are many possible approaches, methods, and techniques that might help us discover unimagined ways of strategizing, sidestepping, deconstructing, dismantling, and circumventing each limit, and expanding our understanding and skills in subtle aspects of dispute resolution.

What is most important for us to understand is that we need not surrender to any of these perceived limits, but can continue searching for their sources, both inside ourselves and in the dysfunctional systems, conflict cultures, and environments we have created and accepted, sometimes without question. It is important, in doing so, that we *consecrate* our failures to the benefit of those who will come after; that we transform our limits into invitations into learning, insight, and improvement; and that we never cease trying to unearth or invent more advanced understandings, improved techniques, and more satisfying relationships.

22

CHALLENGES IN CREATING A CONFLICT REVOLUTION

There are two classes of people who tell what is going to happen in the future: those who don't know and those who don't know they don't know.

— JOHN KENNETH GALBRAITH

If we think of the world's future, we always mean where it will be if it keeps going as we see it going now and it doesn't occur to us that it is not going in a straight line but in a curve, constantly changing direction.

— LUDWIG WITTGENSTEIN

In a revolution, as in a novel, the most difficult part to invent is the end.

— ALEXIS DE TOCQUEVILLE

A s individuals, groups, and societies, we design our futures —
but not always consciously, or entirely as we choose. The
freedom to do so, as the German philosopher Hegel recognized,
resides in our "control over ourselves and over external nature, a
control founded on knowledge of natural necessity; it is therefore
necessarily a product of historical development."

Our ability to consciously design the future of mediation can
therefore be said to depend both on our *internal* awareness, insight,
and skills in mediation; and on our shared understanding of the
external nature of our social, economic, political, and environmental
conflicts, and the roles we might possibly play in resolving them. In
this sense, we can describe the future of mediation as *itself* mediated
and negotiated — in part by our diverse visions, values, attitudes,
intentions, skills, and states of awareness; and in part by our
relationship to the natural and historical conditions in which we live,
imagine, and act. For these reasons, it is nearly impossible for us to
bring about a future for which the internal and external
preconditions have yet to arise, or to imagine a realistic future for
mediation until we have practiced and explored it over an extended
period, learned its deepest lessons, experienced its limits and
frontiers, played with it, and glimpsed its possibilities and promises.
Trying to imagine a future without these experiences, or a future for
which there is inadequate infrastructure, or one that lies beyond the
range of what is possible, leads easily to fantasy and utopianism.
While the French poet Lamartine observed that "utopias are often
only premature truths," permitting even the wildest fantasies to
reveal hidden possibilities, designing an *actual* future for mediation
will require us to link our deepest practical ideas, experiences, and
understandings with a set of theories and design criteria that
describe a kind of future that is both possible and one we would
want to live in.

Ten Limits on What is Possible

If we want to avoid idly fantasizing about the future of mediation,
we need to clarify the *limits* on what it is possible for us to design

and achieve. These limits flow not only from our imprecise ideas about conflict and the future, but our evolving experiences, attitudes, and emotions regarding conflicts in the past and present, where we face immense difficulties and challenges, and where our individual and collective choices can reveal or obscure the alternative futures we seek.

As individuals, groups, societies, and nation states, we jostle for position, fight, make up, adapt, and evolve, and have done so repeatedly throughout history. To consider how we might do so more constructively and successfully in the future, we need to consider the *intrinsic* constraints our experiences of conflict place on our ability to imagine and design alternative futures or alter our attitudes and improve our skills in conflict resolution. Here is a list of my top ten:

1. The nature of mediation, and all forms of dispute resolution, is circumscribed in the first place by the nature of the *conflicts* it seeks to resolve. As mediation is an *operation* performed on conflict, it is initially conflict that shapes mediation, then it is mediation that shapes conflict. Therefore, our ability to invent alternative forms of resolution depends initially on the depth of our understanding of the nature of conflict.

2. Conflict and resolution are dual, opposing, interacting processes like light and dark, good and evil, positive and negative, in which one side can *never* entirely prevail over its opposite, unless both disappear and are transcended. Instead, they continually interact and mutually evolve into more complex, higher order relationships with fresh, emergent, higher order characteristics that cannot be imagined from lower order perspectives. For this reason, resolution can never completely vanquish conflict — nor should it, as conflict is *generative*, and a necessary source and byproduct of change.

3. There are far more ways of creating conflicts, dividing people, and breaking trust than there are of resolving conflicts, uniting people, and building trust. Consequently,

there is a *social* second law of thermodynamics, a kind of *"relational* entropy" that permits resolution only at the cost of increased effort. This can result in *local* complexity and evolution to higher order outcomes, including processes, relationships, and forms of organization, along with a net gain in simplicity and disorganization over time, as disorder is dissipated and exported into the environment.

4. Conflict is classically chaotic, "sensitively dependent on initial conditions," and therefore unpredictable in the long run, allowing small shifts in seemingly insignificant parameters to result in vastly different outcomes. This gives rise to a "mediation butterfly effect," in which apparently trivial actions that result in resolution in one area can give rise to a significant easing of tensions elsewhere.

5. Human conflicts have universal features that make them susceptible — not just to small-scale, one-off efforts, but to large-scale collaborative, systemic, and *strategic* interventions. At the same time, because conflicts are naturally subjective, chaotic, and fluid; and because every mediator is different and works differently, every mediation follows a somewhat unique path, and each moment in mediation diverges from potential others based on the constantly evolving states of mind of the parties and the mediator. The future of mediation is therefore shaped *both* by the nature and character of the unified sum of all our separate conflicts, and by the similarly unified sum of all our subjective experiences in seeking to resolve them.

6. The number and severity of human conflicts has gradually declined over millennia, as Steven Pinker demonstrated in *The Better Angels of our Nature*, suggesting an overall increase in the effectiveness of efforts at communication, collaboration, and conflict resolution. There is no reason to think this trend will decline, and every reason to assume it will continue, perhaps at a more rapid rate as we learn to resolve conflicts more effectively.

7. At the same time, as human populations increase and global

travel, communication, and economic activity expand, greater pressures will be placed on scarce resources, environmental sustainability, and a sensitive ecological balance that will predictably boost the number, severity, and costs of social, economic, political, and environmental conflict. With these, but inevitably lagging a little behind, is our understanding of the growing necessity and importance of jointly solving problems and resolving disputes without costly wars or lengthy litigation.

8. Human responses to conflict are fundamentally shaped by neurophysiological structures and processes that are hard-wired in the brain. These include dual, intertwined conflict pathways, each mediated by a different neurotransmitter, resulting in fundamentally opposing conflict behaviors. Thus, there is an adversarial "fight or flight" pathway mediated by adrenalin, resulting in fear, anger, and aggression; and there is a collaborative "tend and befriend" pathway mediated by oxytocin, resulting in trust, caring, and collaboration. While these pathways are given, neuroscience offers dozens of ways mediators can "nudge," "prime, " and influence which pathway people are likely to choose.

9. Every mediative practice, approach, and style works in some conflicts, but none works always, everywhere, for everyone, or at all times. Yet because the smallest conflicts share features with the largest, and the most unique and particular with the most common and general, *all* techniques, methods, and styles of dispute resolution can contribute to a better understanding of the others, and deepen our skills in navigating the process as a whole.

10. We continuously evolve – not only as individuals, couples, families, and groups, but as organizations, societies, economies, polities, and environments. And we do so *especially* in the nature of our conflicts and approaches to resolution, as we move from simple to more complex, nuanced, and successful practices. In order to more *fully* evolve, we need to improve our skills in resolving not only

particular conflicts, but their veiled logic, underlying coda, chronic character, systemic aspects, ecological interconnections, and binding principles, together with the *latent* lessons they took place in order to teach us.

Ten Links in Constructing a Logical Chain

The extraordinary, deeply moving experience of mediating and assisting thousands of people in resolving conflicts over a diverse array of issues for four decades has led me to a number of understandings regarding the nature of dispute resolution that have been helpful in guiding my practice and shaping my sense of what the future of mediation might look like.

If we want to think more rigorously about the future of mediation and its potential application to a full range of conflicts, *especially* social, economic, political, and environmental disputes, we need to build on the ideas outlined above, start from first principles, and construct a logical chain that is grounded in a set of fundamental ideas, or "axioms" of conflict. Here are my top ten suggestions for constructing such a chain:

1. Every conflict takes place not only between people, but in a *context*, culture, and environment; surrounded by social, economic, and political forces; inside a family, neighborhood, group, or organization; impacted by systems and structures; within a diverse community of people; at a particular moment in time and history, in a specific location in space and geography; on a stage; against a backdrop; in a setting or milieu.

2. None of these elements is conflict-neutral. Each contributes, often in veiled and unspoken, yet profound ways, to the nature, intensity, duration, impact, and *meaning* of our conflicts. Each of these follows a "geodesic" line across the curved, internal space of caring. And each, depending on circumstances, can play a determining role in the success of

the conversations, processes, interventions, and methods we use to prevent, resolve, transform, and transcend them.

3. Nearly *any* complex social, economic, political, or environmental issue can trigger or aggravate conflicts that are internal and personal, relational and interpersonal, or systemic and contextual. Indeed, social inequalities, economic inequities, political imbalances, and environmental disparities are nearly always *experienced* internally and personally, or relationally and interpersonally, leaving the systems and contexts that routinely reproduce them in the shadows, unnoticed and unresolved.

4. Most social, economic, political, and environmental differences, by reason of their internal contradictions, embattled histories, and win/lose assumptions, generate *chronic* conflicts, and with them, *cultures* of conflict avoidance, accommodation, and aggression. These cultures contribute to the rise of a set of adversarial attitudes, coerced compromises, and defensive behaviors regarding social, economic, political, and environmental problems that limit the ability of individuals, families, organizations, and nation states to work collaboratively and democratically, even in small ways, to resolve and transform their differences, design alternative futures, and prevent and transcend their conflicts at their source.

5. Every conflict possesses elements and characteristics that are *fractally* organized, or self-similar on all scales, allowing common attitudes, emotions, ideas, and behaviors to connect what appear to be purely internal conflicts with those that emerge interpersonally in relationships, families, communities, organizations, and societies, and are valid both for children on playgrounds and the heads of nation-states. This self-similarity on all scales allows us to identify ways of adapting techniques that have proven successful in resolving disputes on one level to those that occur on an entirely different level.

6. Nearly all conflicts, no matter how petty or personal, possess veiled social, economic, political, and environmental elements that inform their evolution and eventual outcome. These include, for example, *social* stereotyping, discrimination, and prejudice, which are reflected in our attitudes toward our opponents; *economic* selfishness, callousness, and greed, which are reflected in our unwillingness to compromise or collaborate over financial issues; *political* hierarchies, bureaucracies, and autocracies, which are reflected in the divisive ways we make social decisions, even in the smallest conflicts; and *environmental* exploitation, devastation, and disregard, which are reflected in our destructiveness, insensitivity, and blindness to the ecological consequences of our actions.

7. Even in superficially personal and interpersonal conflicts, and within couples and families, people may be deeply impacted by social, economic, political, and environmental forces. They may, for example, adopt stereotypes or form prejudices and biases against each other. They may be influenced by differences in their status, wealth, power, or work environments. They may quarrel over social expectations, compete for scarce resources, disagree over the way decisions are made, or fight about responsibility for the environmental conditions in which they live. They may support or resist future changes, celebrate or denigrate their prior history, critique or defend the status quo, behave bureaucratically or anarchically regarding rules, and exercise their power democratically or autocratically. Each of these potential sources of individual and interpersonal discord conceals what we can regard as subtle social, economic, political, or environmental characteristics or elements that can leave their conflicts more or less open to resolution, and shift them either in the direction of impasse, intractability, and chronic repetition; or of resolution, plasticity, and prevention.

8. Except when social, economic, political, and environmental issues are *explicitly* addressed in conflict conversations, it is

rare that these contextual, systemic, and ecological elements are openly acknowledged, identified, discussed, or resolved, either by the parties or their mediators. Instead, they linger in the background, generating distortions and misunderstandings that make matters worse; or remain hidden, and as a result, become blockages and sources of resistance that *appear* intractable because we do not know how to address them skillfully.

9. When these aspects of conflict are acknowledged, identified, analyzed, and addressed, they can be transformed into fertile sources of technique and methods for facilitating successful resolutions, transforming communications and relationships, preventing future disputes, and transcending chronic conflicts at their social, economic, political, and environmental sources through learning, collaborative design, and systemic improvement.

10. As a consequence of this logic, nearly any conflict can trigger transformational, *revolutionary* changes that impact not only individuals, couples, and families; but groups and communities, organizations and institutions, cultures and societies, economies and polities, and lead to insights into ways mediation might be *dramatically* expanded and successfully applied — not merely to social, economic, political, and environmental hostilities, which would itself be immensely useful and significant — but to the *design* of social, economic, political, and environmental systems and strutuctures, process and relationships, languages and cultures, attitudes and assumptions, in ways that make them far more effective in preventing and resolving conflicts.

Resolving Chronic, Systemic Conflicts

We can therefore see that every conflict system, context, culture, and environment is fundamentally *grounded* in, characterized by, and oriented to a set of power-, rights- or interest-based systems and structures, processes and relationships, languages and cultures, attitudes and assumptions, each of which requires successively higher levels of skill and permits successively higher orders of resolution that can occur internally or personally, relationally or interactively, and systemically or environmentally.

Our most serious social, economic, political, and environmental conflicts are *chronic,* or repeating, and flow from systemic patterns and sources that are grounded in zero sum power- or rights-based assumptions that fundamentally shape, stall, and sidetrack resolution efforts by restricting them to lower-order models, processes, and methods of resolution. These lower order power- and rights-based social, economic, political, and environmental systems, while designed partly to prevent and resolve conflicts, often do so in rough, primitive, counter-productive, and unskillful ways.

Conflict resolution systems design offers ways of identifying the underlying chronic and systemic sources of social, economic, political, and environmental conflicts, allowing us to design higher order *interest*-based alternatives that can prevent and resolve disputes more rapidly, cheaply, thoroughly, and satisfactorily than power- or rights-based alternatives.

We can elaborate these ideas, experiences, understandings, and design options into a set of proposals for the future development and expansion of dispute resolution; yet, when considered together, they point in a unique, *unified* direction, toward what I call a "conflict revolution," in which mediative principles and systems design methods enable us to fundamentally transform our approaches to chronic conflicts *everywhere.*

Not only is it possible for us to prevent and dramatically reduce the levels of chronic conflict within any given system using conflict resolution systems design methods, it is possible to do so *globally* as well as locally; and to build conflict resolution capacity across and beyond the borders we have invented to defend ourselves from the hostile power- and rights-based, adversarial, win/lose actions of others. Our survival and wellbeing as a *species* increasingly depend on our ability to do so.

In the case of chronic social, economic, political, and environmental conflicts, the ideas and reflections we draw from ordinary mediation practice enable us to design better, grander, more effective, inclusive, and comprehensive dispute resolution systems, techniques, and processes that prioritize the use of interest-based methods in addressing much larger-scale social, economic, political, and environmental differences.

To begin this process, it is important to consider: what exactly are chronic conflicts? I believe they can be defined as those that individuals, couples, families, neighbors, schools, organizations, cultures, societies, economies, and nations:

- Have not fully resolved
- Need to resolve in order to grow and evolve
- Are capable of resolving
- Can only resolve by abandoning old approaches and adopting new ones
- Are resistant to resolving because they are frightened, dissatisfied, insecure, uncertain, angry, or unwilling to change

Chronic conflicts can be distinguished by their high rates of repetition and low levels of resolution; tolerance for disrespectful and adversarial behaviors and seeming irrationality; incongruity between high levels of emotion and apparent triviality of the issues over which people are fighting. They are commonly mistaken for accidental misunderstandings, interpersonal miscommunications and personality clashes, and while they appear to be based on idiosyncratic causes and circumstances, which characterize every conflict, their underlying similarities suggest that they are not only substantively unique, but also patterned responses to underlying systemic causes.

Over the course of centuries, we can identify a number of "meta-sources" of chronic social, economic, political, and environmental conflict. Here again is my personal top ten list:

1. Social inequality
2. Economic inequity
3. Political autocracy
4. Environmental disregard and ecological destructiveness
5. Stereotyping, prejudice, bias and discrimination
6. Hyper-competitive organizations and economic greed
7. Hierarchy, bureaucracy, graft and corruption
8. Power and rights based systems, processes and relationships
9. Aggressive, win/lose approaches to problem-solving, negotiation and mediation, and avoidant or aggressive conflict cultures
10. Exclusive, one-sided and unilateral approaches to problem solving, decision-making and change

None of these is unavoidable or inevitable. Each can be reduced, resolved, transformed, transcended, and prevented once we understand its *apparent* necessity and underlying motivation. While there are others, none of these meta-sources is currently being addressed using advanced conflict resolution techniques — partly because they are complex, multi-faceted, and difficult to resolve; partly because they require fresh, innovative solutions; and partly because we have not explained how fundamental, far-reaching transformations in our responses to these sources of conflict might actually be possible.

In my view, it is well within the power of existing conflict resolution methodologies to invent, design, and implement at least *partial* solutions to all these problems – not through dictatorial imposition, adversarial rhetoric, and one-sided power- and rights-based approaches; but through democratic dialogue, collaborative deliberation, systems design, and the multi-sided approaches of interest-based dispute resolution methodologies.

By learning how to prevent, resolve, transform, transcend, and prevent conflicts within the relatively constrained context of interpersonal disputes, we can discover a much larger truth regarding the future of mediation: that it is *possible* for us to evolve to a higher social order than domination and inequality; a higher economic order than selfishness and short-term advantage; a higher political order than autocracy and petty personal attacks; and a higher environmental order than climate change denial and species extinction.

More profoundly, through mediation *practice* it is possible to perceive that there are higher orders *both* of conflict *and* resolution; that we cannot fully comprehend conflicts in general, or *completely* resolve or overcome particular disputes, no matter how trivial or inconsequential, without also addressing the subtle influence, even in couples and families, of biases and inequalities in status; inequities and unfairnesses in wealth; autocratic and domineering uses of power; or exploitative and abusive environmental practices, which directly and indirectly shape the ways we understand discord and respond to it.

As we develop more skillful and effective methods for resolving individual and interpersonal conflicts, we may then realize that, with a bit of tweaking, it is possible to apply them also to schools and workplaces, neighborhoods and communities, organizations and institutions. From there, it is not difficult to imagine how we might apply similarly scaled-up, suitably modified methods to global social, economic, political, and environmental conflicts.

Doing so will demand not only that we take a collaborative, integrative, non-violent, and *appreciative* approach to diversity and dissent, and thus to conflict, leading us to seek out the systemic sources of chronic hostility and antagonism; but that we realize that *every* conflict experience and opposing perspective contains *some* truth that can be reframed or reconfigured in ways that allow it to be understood even by its most ardent opponents, and contribute to the implementation of improved, synergistic, collaborative, global solutions.

This is not meant to imply that all points of view are equally factually or scientifically correct, but that beneath all the competing facts and scientific explanations lie human interests and desires, expectations and assumptions, emotions and experiences, myths and stories, novels and poems, songs and dances, *all* of which can be true at the same time. This entails a shift from zero sum to non-zero sum processes, from fixed hierarchies to fluid heterarchies, and from power- and rights-based methodologies to interest-based ones.

More profoundly and consequentially, it means that, on a large enough scale, with deep enough empathy and a clear enough understanding, we can move beyond "us versus them" conflicts by realizing, as I suggested earlier, that there *is* no "them," there is just "us." The "them" we create through conflict is simply the flip-side of our own pain and disappointment, our alienation from wholeness, and our lost capacity for empathy and compassion.

These ways of thinking encourage us to imagine how we might fundamentally redesign and *revolutionize* the systems, processes, and relationships; the groups, institutions, and organizations; the cultures, contexts, and values; even the language, stories and narratives we create to interact and resolve conflicts – and not just individually and interpersonally, but socially, economically, politically, and environmentally, using the systems design process to shift from power- and rights-based methods to interest-based ones.

Criteria for Systems Design Processes

In considering how we might design dispute resolution systems for social, economic, political, and environmental conflicts, it is helpful to begin by appreciating that dispute resolution, for the most part, follows certain generic rules or guidelines, adheres to particular patterns and forms, and embodies a set of shared values or principles. It is possible for these rules, patterns, and values to be expressed directly in the form of *design criteria* – i.e., as a kind of algorithm or procedure that can, through a series of steps, produce roughly anticipatable results.

These generic criteria, as discussed in Chapter 19, appear to me to contain the following fifteen elements:

1. All interested parties are included and invited to participate

fully in designing and implementing content, process, and relationships.

2. Decisions are made by consensus wherever possible, and nothing is considered final until everyone is in agreement.

3. Diversity and honest differences are viewed as sources of dialogue, leading to better ideas, healthier relationships, and greater unity.

4. Stereotypes, prejudices, assumptions of innate superiority, and ideas of intrinsic correctness are considered divisive and discounted as one-sided descriptions of more complex, multi-sided, paradoxical realities.

5. Openness, authenticity, appreciation, and empathy are regarded as better foundations for communication and decision-making than secrecy, rhetoric, insult, and demonization.

6. Dialogue and open-ended questions are deemed more useful than debate and cross-examination.

7. Force, violence, coercion, aggression, humiliation, and domination are rejected, both as methods and as outcomes.

8. Cooperation and collaboration are ranked as primary, while competition and aggression are considered secondary.

9. Everyone's interests are accepted as legitimate, acknowledged, and satisfied wherever possible, consistent with others' interests.

10. Processes and relationships are considered at least as important as content, if not more so.

11. Attention is paid to emotions, subjectivity, and feelings, as well as to logic, objectivity, and facts.

12. Everyone is regarded as responsible for participating in improving content, processes, and relationships, and searching for synergies and transformations.

13. People are invited into heartfelt communications and self-awareness, and encouraged to reach resolution, forgiveness, and reconciliation.

14. Chronic conflicts are traced to their systemic sources, where

they can be prevented and redesigned to discourage repetition.

15. Victory is regarded as obtainable by everyone, and redirected toward collaborating to solve common problems, so that no one feels defeated.

These rules, patterns, and values can be adapted, tweaked, and modified to fit particular conflicts and issues; or, they can help initiate and guide a larger dispute resolution systems design process; or, they can aid in evaluating existing resolution procedures to see how they might be improved. In these ways, mediators can significantly alter the course of chronic conflicts — for example, by inviting people to speak directly to each other about their experiences, perceptions, and expectations; or their angers and fears, unspoken desires, requests for dignity and respect, love for one another, or their aspirations to solve the problems they care about most deeply. Doing so in political conflicts will require extraordinary ingenuity, commitment, and complex, higher order skills--but these are *exactly* the skills we need to resolve any chronic conflict, draw people into dialogue, and keep relationships alive, and are well worth practicing whatever effort it takes.

How Do We Know if a Better Political Future Is Even Possible?

If we want to design a future for mediation that acknowledges our limitations and builds on our experiences, it is important to have a clear sense, not only that non-zero sum, egalitarian, respectful, democratic, interest-based approaches are better than their zero sum, condescending, autocratic, power- and rights-based cousins, but *why* they are better, and how we can bring them into existence.

It is easy to demonstrate that there are worthier outcomes than winning and losing, more successful processes than shaming and blaming, and deeper relationships than exercising power over and against others. These outcomes are achieved when everyone's interests have been heard and addressed or satisfied; when adversaries engage in meaningful dialogue and creatively solve their common problems; when they collaboratively negotiate win/win agreements; when they search for just, *restorative* outcomes, rather than one-sided, retributive ones; when power is exercised *with* and *for* others rather than *over* and *against* them; and when everyone genuinely feels they have won.

These are not utopian fantasies, idealistic dreams, or wishful thinking, but the regular and repeated result of thousands of mediators successfully applying interest-based techniques to a wide variety of disputes in diverse communities around the world over several decades. The methodologies that have proven most successful, in my view, include these twenty or so:

1. Active, empathetic, and responsive listening
2. Joint, informal, creative problem solving
3. Collaborative negotiation and win/win bargaining
4. Nonviolent communication, appreciative inquiry, mindfulness, and emotional intelligence
5. Small and large group facilitation
6. Consensus building and impasse resolution
7. Dialogue facilitation and public policy mediation
8. Circles, restorative justice, and victim-offender mediation
9. Conflict coaching and trauma informed mediation
10. Bias awareness, prejudice reduction, and cross-cultural mediation
11. School and peer mediation
12. Neighborhood, community and environmental mediation
13. Organizational Ombuds offices
14. Conflict resolution consulting
15. Grievance, workplace and collective bargaining mediation
16. Prenuptial, marital, and relationship mediation
17. Divorce mediation and collaborative practice
18. Conflict resolution systems design
19. Multidoor courthouses, commercial, and litigated mediation
20. Truth and reconciliation commissions and forgiveness practices

At the core of all these methodologies is the recognition that opportunities for improved outcomes and relationships flow *precisely* from our differences; that we can overcome selfishness and defensiveness through listening, consensus building, and collaborative negotiation; that we can forgive ourselves and each other for what we have done; that we can rekindle the ability to empathize with our opponents, learn from our conflicts, reconcile and repair our relationships, and reopen our hearts to one another.

These outcomes are deepened and made more lasting when we move *beyond* even resolution, forgiveness, and reconciliation to prevention, and collaboratively redesign the dysfunctional systems and environments, organizations and institutions, processes and relationships, narratives and cultures that generated or aggravated our disputes. This requires us to jointly and proactively search for ways of preventing similar difficulties from arising in the future; and encourage, expand, and strengthen conflict resolution skills and capacities *everywhere*.

This, I believe, is what a "conflict revolution" might look like, and a very real possibility for what our future could become, if we are able to imagine, design, and practice it on large- as well as small-scales. In conflict resolution, it is common to discover that these scales are connected, and to see that every large, seemingly complicated issue, like respect, boils down to some small, deceptively simple behavior, like saying "thank you."

This suggests that any genuine revolution in our approach to conflict and resolution will necessarily challenge all of us — not only personally and relationally, but socially, economically, politically, and environmentally. What, then, are some of these challenges, and how might we rise to meet them?

Our Challenges

Our first challenge in seeking to design a future for mediation is to *imagine* it. Imagination is a precious resource, as we tend to imagine what we already know, and find it difficult to imagine what we have never experienced. Nonetheless, as Greek novelist Nikos Kazantzakis reminded us,

> By believing passionately in something that still does not exist, we create it. The non-existent is whatever we have not sufficiently desired.

Our second challenge is to dare to create the future we desire, starting of course with the tiny steps each of us can take every day to bring it into existence. These steps become easier when we realize, with Albert Camus, that "Real generosity toward the future consists in giving everything you have to the present."

Meeting these first two challenges forces us to face a third, and figure out how to connect what we imagine with the steps we can take everyday. This will require us to synthesize the very small, simple, *practical* problems we face in resolving individual, interpersonal, and organizational conflicts, with the very large, complex, *theoretical* lessons we derive from identifying the chronic and systemic sources of social, economic, political, and environmental conflicts. This will allow us to initiate an innovative, collaborative, *revolutionary* redesign of chronically conflicted social, economic, political, and environmental practices; and to consider how we might build a broad array of mediative mechanisms into the daily operations of *all* our systems, structures, processes, relationships, languages, and cultures.

The mere *idea* that conflict resolution principles could make social institutions less adversarial, ameliorate the chronic sources of economic hostility, reduce the costs of adversarial political disputes, and encourage deeper, cheaper, longer lasting environmental resolutions is reason enough for us to focus our energy and attention on what may be required to do so. Yet to *actually* undertake this task will pose a number of additional unique and profound challenges for anyone seeking to design a better future.

One such challenge will be to discover how we might use conflict resolution theories and practices to gain fresh insights into the reasons social, economic political, and environmental disputes become so adversarial and intractable. This will lead us to develop a rich set of options for preventing and resolving them, and hopefully become more effective in halting the senseless and disheartening destruction of individuals and communities, brutalization of life, loss of pleasure and enjoyment, and debilitating waste and misery experienced by countless people in conflict every day around the world.

A further challenge will be to discover, in reverse, whether we can use social, economic, political, and environmental principles to clarify the systemic factors that contribute to impasse in what appear to be purely personal or interpersonal conflicts. This will allow us to plumb a rich array of sociological methods, economic analyses, political theories, and ecological understandings for innovative ways of deepening and sustaining dispute resolution processes in other conflicts.

An additional challenge will be to discover how we might collaborate across racial, gender, religious, class, and similar differences in applying conflict resolution systems design principles to the root causes of these disputes, and *design* from first principles an interactive set of approaches that will be more successful in resolving, transforming, transcending and preventing them. Doing so will permit us to evolve to higher orders of conflict and resolution than we think are even possible.

A significantly deeper challenge will be to clarify the human, heart-based, and "spiritual" values that inform our understanding and participation in conflict resolution, and elucidate the techniques that produce its most profound, poignant, and far-reaching successes. This will enable us to ground the entire process in heartfelt desires for connection, which inform all collaborative, interest-based processes, and to anchor them at the center of our social, economic, political, and environmental lives. This will encourage us to invent more humane ways of solving planetary problems across the countless differences that divide us.

An immensely useful challenge will be to genuinely understand that *every* conflict is simply the sound made by the cracks in a system, the voice of the new paradigm, and a call for change in a system that has outlived its usefulness. It is is a shallow, superficial response to differences, diversity, and dissent that ignores their importance in creating balance, synergy, and symbiosis in systems, and improves our success in solving problems. Every conflict is therefore *automatically* an opportunity, an invitation, and a *request* for improvement.

A difficult challenge will be to assist conflicted parties in recognizing that their ability to become an integrated and authentic *Self* internally rests on their ability to accept and celebrate the diversity of *Others* externally, and therefore on their ability to appreciate the importance of diversity, complexity, uncertainty, ambiguity, non-conformity, disagreement, and self-determination in designing the systems that reward or punish these behaviors. These understandings, in turn, ask us not to forget that we are all integral elements in a living environment, and inseparable from it. Ourselves, others, and nature may *appear* divided and distinct, but in essence, we are united and one.

A more serious challenge will be to try to bring about these revolutionary changes without triggering reactive conflicts, or using power- or right-based change processes that merely harden resistance to what most needs improving. Doing so will challenge us to find new ways of improving highly complex and deeply entrenched global systems, and to recognize the enduring validity of Gandhi's insight that we need to "*be* the change we want to see in the world." As writer Michael Ventura described it, "The future lives in our individual, often lonely, and certainly unprofitable acts of integrity, or it doesn't live at all."

A broader challenge will be to meet all of these challenges both locally *and* globally, and initiate international, multi-track, personal and online collaborations to assist neighboring countries and communities in doing the same. This will encourage us to recognize that conflicts *have* no borders, and can quickly spread across those we imagine to impact all of us. We may then commit to working more actively and conscientiously to increase conflict resolution capacity internationally across cultures and imaginary divides.

A significant challenge will be to be *audacious* enough to act as global citizens and "conflict revolutionists;" to have the courage to take on the world and imagine how it might be better — and at the same time, be humble enough to acknowledge our imperfections, appreciate the danger of meddling with what we don't fully understand, and realize that, in the end, it is *we* who create our conflicts, and ourselves who most need changing.

A closing challenge will be to face all of these challenges open-heartedly. As Joseph Campbell aptly expressed it, we can "participate joyfully in the sorrows of the world." We may not be able to fix what is ailing, or rid the world of its sorrows, but we are always able to improve our *attitudes*, even in the midst of the worst conflicts. Victor Frankl movingly wrote, based on his concentration camp experiences during World War II, that "Everything can be taken from a man but … the last of human freedoms – to chose one's attitude in any given set of circumstances, to choose one's own way."

More than anything, mediation fundamentally consist of an attitude, perspective, or approach to conflict that genuinely regards it as an *adventure*, a gift, an opportunity for learning and improvement, an invitation to design a future that is less conflicted than the past. Charles Swindol described the extraordinary experience of realizing that we can change our lives simply by changing our attitude:

> The longer I live, the more I realize the impact of attitude on life. Attitude, to me is more basic than facts. It is more important than the past, than education, than money, than circumstances, than failures, than successes, than what other people think or say or do. It is more important than appearance, giftedness or skill. It will make or break a company … a church … a home. The remarkable thing is we have a choice every day regarding the attitude we will embrace for that day. We cannot change our past … we cannot change the fact that people will act in a certain way. We cannot change the inevitable. The only

thing we can do is play on the one string we have, and that is our attitude. I am convinced that life is 10 percent what happens to me and 90 percent how I react to it. And so, it is with you ... we are in charge of our attitudes.

Simply by seeking to meet these challenges, we *invite* the future into existence, simultaneously within, between, and around us. And we can do so every day, in every conflict, moment-by-moment, by shifting our attitudes and the choices we make, as mediators and as parties. The eminent historian Howard Zinn, summarizing centuries of conflict, concluded:

> We don't have to wait for some grand utopian future. The future is an infinite succession of presents, and to live now as we think human beings should live, in defiance of all that is bad around us, is itself a marvelous victory.

Instead of waiting for some far-off day when a less conflicted future may miraculously appear, we can give birth to it by living it every day, as best we can. As "cyberpunk" author William Gibson astutely observed, "The future is already here; it's just not evenly distributed." We can foresee the future in miniature in every mediation. All we need to do is figure out how to redistribute it.

ABOUT THE AUTHOR

Kenneth Cloke is Director of the Center for Dispute Resolution and for over forty years has been a mediator, arbitrator, facilitator, coach, consultant and trainer, specializing in communication, negotiation, and resolving complex multi-party disputes, including marital, divorce, family, community, grievance and workplace disputes, collective bargaining negotiations, organizational and school conflicts, sexual harassment, discrimination, and public policy disputes; and designing preventative conflict resolution systems.

His facilitation, coaching, consulting, and training practice includes work with leaders of public, private and non-profit organizations on effective communications, dialogue, collaborative negotiation, relationship and team building, conflict resolution, leadership development, strategic planning, designing systems, culture and organizational change.

His university teaching includes mediation, law, history, political science, conflict studies, urban studies, and other topics at several colleges and universities. He is or has recently been an Adjunct Professor at Pepperdine University School of Law; Southern Methodist University; USC, Global Negotiation Insight Institute at Harvard Law School; Omega Institute; Albert Einstein College of Medicine, Cape Cod Institute; University of Amsterdam ADR Institute; Saybrook University; Massey University (New Zealand).

He has done conflict resolution work in Armenia, Australia, Austria, Bahamas, Brazil, Canada, China, Cuba, Denmark, England, Georgia, Greece, India, Ireland, Japan, Mexico, Netherlands, New Zealand, Nicaragua, Pakistan, Puerto Rico, Scotland, Slovenia, Spain, Thailand, Turkey, Ukraine, USSR, and Zimbabwe. He is founder and first President of Mediators Beyond Borders.

He served as an Administrative Law Judge for the California Agricultural Labor Relations Board and the Public Employment Relations Board, a Factfinder for the Public Employment Relations Board, and a Judge *Pro Tem* for the Superior Court of Los Angeles. He has been an Arbitrator and Mediator for over forty years in labor management disputes, and is a member of a number of arbitration panels.

He received his B.A. from the University of California, Berkeley; J.D. from U.C. Berkeley's Boalt Law School; Ph.D. from U.C.L.A.; LLM from U.C.L.A. Law School; and did post-doctoral work at Yale University School of Law. He is a graduate of the National Judicial College and has taken graduate level courses in a variety of subjects.

INDEX

Index